MANAGING HUMAN RESOURCES:

A STRATEGIC PERSPECTIVE

by James R. Nininger

A Report Published by the Compensation
Research Centre of The Conference Board
of Canada, April 1982

Contents

Exhibits

Appendices

Foreword

Human resources have been long considered one of the most important of an organization's resources. Much progress has been made over the years in developing policies and programs to assist in the management of these resources. Operationally speaking, many organizations have efficient and effective human resource management systems in place.

There has been a gap, however, at the more strategic level where progress at integrating the management of human resources with overall strategic planning and management of the enterprise has not kept pace with operational developments. Because of this, there have been instances of crises management; and responses to unforeseen changes have led to inefficiencies in overall organizational performance. This study is designed to help close this gap by presenting a set of principles, which will serve as guidelines to link more effectively human resource management with organizational strategy. Also presented are examples and case histories to supplement these guidelines.

The senior human resource executives of ten Canadian organizations provided the initiative for this study, which is the result of their collaborative effort with the staff of The Conference Board of Canada. Chief executive officers from a number of these organizations also contributed. The seven principles evolved over a period of two years during which many meetings were held where experiences were shared and the principles frequently tested. The names of these senior human resource executives with their organizational affiliation are listed below. In some cases, the senior executive was assisted by another individual whose name also appears:

Alcan Aluminium Limited	H. Stewart Ladd
Bell Canada	Harry Pilkington, John A. McCutcheon
Canadian General Electric Company Limited	H. W. Johnson, P. Tuck
Canadian National	K. E. Hunt, A. E. Deegan
Celanese Canada Inc.	Emile J. Carrière
The Molson Companies Ltd.	H. E. C. Stoneham, G. C. Taylor

Northern Telecom Limited	D. A. Noble
Polysar Limited	H. A. Graham
Shell Canada Limited	W. A. M. Birt
Steinberg Inc.	Henri Tremblay

J.D. Belford, now retired, also played a very important role in both initiating and taking part in the research. The contributions of these individuals made this study possible and their time and effort are gratefully acknowledged.

Support for the study was provided by the Compensation Research Centre, a separately funded division of The Conference Board of Canada, which carries out research into key compensation issues and activities related to the management of human resources.

James R. Nininger
President
The Conference Board of Canada   April 1982

Author's Acknowledgments

The author would like to express his appreciation to a number of individuals at The Conference Board of Canada who assisted in publishing the report: Louis Julien, who compiled information and co-ordinated the logistics for the research; Patricia Sims, who typed the original draft of the study and assisted in administering other aspects of the project; the staff of the Word Processing Centre, who produced numerous drafts of the study; Ruth Kirkpatrick, who prepared the diagrams; Steve Bain, who designed the cover artwork; and Robert Albota, who served as technical editor of the report.

Executive Summary

This study examines the link between human resource management and overall organizational strategy. Its aim is to provide guidelines that will be useful in exploring ways of improving the management of this increasingly vital linkage.

The need to examine this relationship has occurred for two reasons. First, there has been increasing awareness among many executives that human resources should be managed with the same strategic or future-oriented focus as physical and capital resources. Second, changes in the work place, whether they be driven by economic, social, technological or political forces, are likely to intensify. Thus, organizational vitality, and perhaps even survival, require a more strategic approach to the management of human resources.

Background

The study had its origins in 1979. A number of senior human resource executives, meeting under the auspices of The Conference Board of Canada, believed that although the various techniques available for the management of human resources were fairly well developed a gap in knowledge existed at the more strategic level, specifically in dealing with the linkage between long-term human resource planning and strategic planning and management. Over the course of the next two years, these individuals, from ten different organizations, met to share experiences and to develop a set of principles or guidelines that would be helpful to others wishing to improve their organizational effectiveness in this area.

Seven principles emerged. While they are based on the experiences of a small number of organizations, it is felt that they are generally applicable and can be adapted to other organizations. This study will make a useful contribution if it provides a basis for encouraging discussions as to whether the areas represented by the principles are being managed effectively.

The Seven Principles

The seven principles are listed below. Each principle should be read with the following preamble: Effective human resource management, in the context of overall business planning and management, is facilitated to the extent that:

1. There is an overall corporate purpose and that the human resource dimensions of that purpose are evident.

2. A process of developing strategy within the organization exists and is understood, and that there is explicit consideration of human resource dimensions.

3. Effective linkages exist on a continuing basis to ensure the integration of human resource considerations with the organizational decision-making processes.

4. The office of the chief executive officer provides the climate for integrating human resource considerations to the needs of the business.

5. The organization at all levels establishes responsibility and accountability for human resource management.

6. Initiatives in the management of human resources are relevant to the needs of the business.

7. It includes the responsibility to identify and interact in the social, political, technological and economic environments in which the organization is and will be doing business.

Principle 1 — Corporate Purpose

Corporate purpose refers to the expression of the basic philosophy that guides the operations of an organization. The first principle argues that basic organizational values and beliefs, including those related to human resources, be carefully articulated, well understood — particularly among senior executives — and practised on an ongoing basis.

An organization could devote time and effort to defining, or reassessing, its philosophy of management when:

- the relevance of the current values and beliefs in an ever changing environment is felt to be inadequate.

- there is an incongruence between corporate values and beliefs and corporate behaviour.

Human resource dimensions of organizational purpose could include values and beliefs about the following: Organizational communication, contributions to organizational effectiveness, individual development and advancement, work and the work environment, expectations of the individual and the organization, reviewing and rewarding performance, etc.

The need for a clearly understood corporate purpose is usually accepted without question; however, it could prove useful to assess the degree to which the values and beliefs of the organization are understood and followed.

Principle 2 — The Strategic Planning Process

Strategic planning deals with the fundamental nature and direction of the organization. The study's second principle states that effective integration of human resources and business planning is dependent upon the existence of a process of developing strategy that is understood at relevant levels of the organization and includes explicit consideration of the human resource dimensions of corporate strategy.

In the past, the human resource aspects of the strategic planning process have tended to be after-the-fact or secondary in nature. The realization that human resource considerations can hinder organizational growth and development has led to the desire to seek improved means of systematically integrating human resources and strategic planning in a consistent and disciplined manner.

This can be accomplished by ensuring that active consideration is given to the organization's human resources in the strategic planning process. That this has been done will be in evidence in the actual plan and in its execution.

Principle 3 — Organizational Linkages

The third principle states that effective linkages should exist on a continuing basis to ensure the integration of human resource considerations with the organizational decision-making processes. Five linkages were examined in the study.

1. *Board of Directors:* The board of directors can play an important role in human resource matters whether it be reviewing, approving or initiating courses of action.

2. *The Senior Executive Level:* Effective ways of ensuring human resource input into the senior executive decision-making processes of the organization should be in place. Three aspects were examined:

   - the senior human resource executive and his role in influencing senior decision-making levels of the organization,

   - the senior management decision-making council of the organization and human resource inputs into its deliberations,

   - other senior management councils that deal with human resource matters such as succession planning forums.

3. *Linkages with Senior Line Managers:* There must be effective working relationships between senior line managers at the corporate and business levels and senior human resource functional managers.

4. *Linkages at Other Organizational Levels:* It is important that effective human resource input into decision making at all other levels of the organization takes place on an ongoing basis.

5. *Functional Integration:* Effective linkages between the corporate human resource functional organization and its counterpart organizational unit at the subsidiary or business unit level should be in place.

Principle 4 — The Office of the Chief Executive Officer

The office of the chief executive officer (CEO) has a very important role to play in providing the climate for integrating human resources with strategic planning and management. The realities of managing complex organizations leads to the desired climate emerging from a more collegial forum of the senior executives in the organization, hence, the use of the term *office*.

The role of the chief executive officer, however, should not be understated. There are many ways he can establish and maintain the desired climate for the organization. These tend to fall into two categories.

1. The use of organizational systems and processes that support the management of human resources. Adherence to the following processes will assist in establishing the appropriate climate:

    - ensuring that human resource considerations are an integral part of strategic and operational planning processes,

    - making effective use of formal and informal methods of organizational communication to relate the CEO's views on human resources,

    - following the established process of performance reviewing,

    - relating performance in the management of human resources to the reward system,

    - managing the organization's succession planning process effectively.

2. The personal style and approach of the chief executive officer has an important impact on the climate in the organization.

The chief executive officer also has an important role to play in establishing and maintaining the desired climate in the human resource function of the organization.

Principle 5 — Establishing Responsibilities for Human Resource Management

The fifth principle states that responsibility and accountability for human resource management should be clearly established at all levels of the organization. The primary responsibility for human resource management rests with line managers throughout the organization.

The organization must establish the proper environment to support this approach and must reinforce it with a variety of methods to assist managers to meet these responsibilities including:

1. *The Business Planning Process.* Proper recognition of human resource objectives in both the strategic and operating plans will assist in providing the framework for establishing responsibility.

2. *The Succession Planning Process.* Succession planning is the responsibility of line managers throughout the organization and the appropriate tools for carrying out this responsibility must be provided.

3. *The Individual Manager Context.* A number of methods can be helpful to individual managers in assisting them to meet their responsibilities in managing their human resources:

   - the use of position descriptions,

   - the establishment of human resource objectives,

   - the rewarding of performance in human resource management.

Principle 6 — Human Resource Initiatives

The sixth principle states that initiatives in the management of human resources should be tied to the objectives and the needs of the business. The principle suggests that it may be desirable to examine the role of the human resource function and to review the responsibilities for human resource management between line managers and human resource functional managers. In this regard some guidelines emerged from the study:

Guidelines Relating to the Role of the Function

- The direction and activities of the function should be geared to meeting the needs of the business.

- There are three dimensions of the role: to provide functional expertise throughout the organization; to provide human resource leadership by ensuring that changes are anticipated and planned for, and to play an effective part in the overall management of the business.

- The organization's environments, both internal and external, must be monitored on an ongoing basis.

Guidelines Relating to Responsibilities

- Ensuring that initiatives reflect the needs of the business are a responsibility of both line managers and human resource functional managers.

- Two needs must be satisfied: to ensure that ongoing human resource systems are operating at high standards, and to ensure that periodic initiatives are undertaken to assist the organization in adapting to its changing environment.

- Operating managers have a right to expect human resource systems to be in place to meet the first need and have a responsibility to do their part to ensure that initiatives are undertaken.

A number of aspects of the management of the human resource function were examined. These included:

- the planning process within the function,

- the structure of the function to meet its mission,

- the blend of skills required in the human resource function at various levels,

- determining the effectiveness of the function.

Principle 7 — Dealing with the Organization's Environments

Organizations operate in a complex and ever changing environmental setting. This last principle suggests that the effective integration of human resource management with the overall management of the organization includes the responsibility to identify and interact in the social, economic, political and technological environments in which the organization is and will be doing business.

Assessing the environment and its possible impact on the organization is not a new phenomenon. Recently, however, there has been heightened interest on the part of many organizations to discover better ways of understanding and dealing with various segments of the environment. To accomplish this environmental monitoring has evolved into an important responsibility for all managers including human resource functional managers. A variety of approaches for organizing effective environmental monitoring were examined. These approaches are not mutually exclusive:

- the senior executive group and its role in systematically focusing on the organization's environments;

- the assignment of responsibilities for gathering and analyzing environmental information to a central monitoring activity;

- the use of the strategic planning process, which should contain a thorough analysis of the business environment;

- ensuring that each organizational function views the monitoring of its relevant environments as one of its key roles.

Accordingly, the human resource function should have clearly identified processes in place to monitor its external and internal environments in order to carry out its responsibilities in identifying and interacting with the internal and external environments.

Some Cautions in Interpreting the Principles

A number of points should be kept in mind when drawing conclusions from a comparison of the seven principles with existing practices in an organization:

- None of the participants in the study would suggest that their organization was coping in all seven areas to an optimal degree. Rather, each felt they were following a number of the principles effectively and were striving to improve their performance in others.

- The seven principles are not intended for use as a checklist that in practice can or should be followed in sequential order. Organizations tend to deal with problems and react to opportunities and will not usually follow a sequence of principles such as presented in this report. Specific principles will have relevance at particular points in time.

- The study does not attempt to establish a relationship between the effectiveness with which human resource planning is integrated into the organization *and* the success or failure of a business. Success or failure is far more complex than a relationship between one set of variables and a particular outcome.

- In general, the participants felt that as an organization reaches a stage of optimal integration of human resource and business planning, it is more likely to take advantage of opportunities that come its way than if the state of integration was minimal.

I A Perspective on Managing Human Resources

The theme of this report is that organizations must be highly effective in the management of their human resources. Organizational vitality and growth — and in some instances survival — will depend on how well this challenge is met. Meeting this challenge requires a strategic orientation to the management of the most important of all resources.

For many organizations, the process of formulating strategy has evolved considerably over the course of the last ten to fifteen years. Initially, planning took place in a period of relatively little change in the economic, social, technological and political environments. In the next phase, planning took place in a period of change in society; however, the changes were more or less predictable. The current phase can be described as a period where economic, social, political and technological conditions are in a constant state of flux. Changes are, in many cases, either harder to predict or are unexpected. Furthermore, these changes have the potential to alter significantly the direction of an organization, sometimes with unfortunate consequences.

Changes in the business environment have originated from many directions, among them changes in the character of the work force and the nature of the work place. In addition, rapidly shifting markets, increased international competition, new and changing technologies, increased government regulations, and uneven patterns of economic growth have all had an impact on the process of strategy formulation and indeed on organizational performance.

As a consequence of these changes, it has been recognized that traditional ways of viewing the management of human resources have been insufficient and in some cases unsatisfactory. The human resource implications of a decision could no longer be relegated to an after-the-fact status, nor the personnel function viewed in the role of "looking after the people side of the business."

Accordingly, human resources have increasingly been viewed as a resource to be managed *strategically* as well as *operationally*. In this sense, human resource planning and management are closely integrated with the overall strategy of the organization. Emerging trends and issues in the human resource environment are identified, their impact analyzed, and managed with the same level of professional competence and business acumen as is applied to other areas of the business. Further, the personnel function itself is managed in a strategic sense and plays an important part in contributing to the overall management of the organization. Organizations that have developed this strategic focus are felt to be in a better position to reap the benefits of their efforts either by being able to take advantage of opportunities that come their way, or by anticipating and dealing with potential problems more effectively.

Two factors have led to the acceptance of this strategic orientation to the management of human resources. The first is that it makes good business sense to manage human resources in the same manner that capital or physical resources are managed. Few would challenge this. What is needed is a framework to help assess existing performance in this area. Providing such a framework, based on the findings of the research, is the main purpose of this study. The second factor relates to continued environmental change. The human resource environments will continue to undergo pervasive changes, which in all likelihood will lead to environments that will be considerably different in the future. It will be necessary to be cognizant of these changes and, more important, to manage them effectively. This will require a strategic and proactive stance. The next section briefly examines a number of these changes and their possible ramifications on organizations.

An Environment in Transition

The overall economic environment is and will continue to undergo change. Lower real growth will likely be a dominant constraint in the future while inflation will persist. This is likely to affect terms and conditions of employment on a whole range of issues including compensation and job security. As well, there will be disparate rates of growth by business sectors and by region. This requires different human resource strategies for lower and higher growth areas. Persistent areas of low growth tend to nurture certain attitudes and approaches to work (collectivism, protection) that are different from the characteristics of higher growth business sectors or regions. This occurs both domestically and internationally.

Another characteristic of the economic environment will be increased global competition and the attendant international markets and world scale operations. These will continue to benefit organizations with a competitive advantage, leading to the shrinking of job opportunities in some of the traditional non-competitive sectors. This has important human resource implications. Shortages of skilled labour will continue to exist in areas of high growth resulting in ample employment opportunities. Job protection will be the focus of concern in uncompetitive sectors. The work force is expected to undergo changes that will have an impact on all organizations, both in terms of its composition as well as in its attitudes and values about work.

In North America, a decline in the overall rate of growth of the labour force will mean a gradually aging work force. Fewer young people entering the labour force will create more competition among employers, which in turn may lead to a re-examination of the kind of work that makes up entry level positions. The aging of the work force will require the effective utilization of older workers, additional retraining programs, and more flexibility in retirement patterns. It may also bring about changes in retirement income. The changing sex composition of the work force towards higher participation of females will continue to be felt in many areas including pressures for flexible work schedules, part-time work, day care facilities, and more liberal maternity benefits. Finally a continued increase in the educational level of the work force may bring about changes in entry level work that could focus more attention on management of the so-called "knowledge worker."

Continued shortages of manpower will exist in specific occupations and specific regions. These shortages may restrict business expansion and may necessitate the adoption of innovative approaches to deal with the problem. As well, it will likely result in increased government attempts to more effectively match the supply and demand for labour. In summary, the North American work force is expected to be better educated and increasingly more mature, with the potential of being very productive. Innovative human resource management approaches will capitalize on the attributes of the work force.

Attitudes towards work and the very meaning of work itself will continue to be in transition. Traditional work-oriented values will be supplanted by values that reflect evolving life styles and perceptions of work. Work, for many, is expected to be less authority oriented and employees will want added input into their work and how it gets done. Organizations will search for ways of humanizing the work environment and improving the quality of working life in jobs at all levels and in all industries. Innovative approaches in employee-employer relations should lead to more effective ways of resolving conflicts.

Changes in technology will continue to revolutionize the work place, leading to a loss of jobs in some cases. In other cases, it will mean retraining employees as well as creating new jobs. Many organizations will be affected by each of these outcomes. Effective resolution of the impact of technological change will require the combined efforts of business, labour, government, education, and other institutions. Finally, increased work place legislation will have a significant impact on all organizations. The protection of the rights of individuals and the correction of real and perceived injustices will require all organizations to keep abreast of these changes and their likely impact.

This brief review of the evolving human resource environments underscores the importance of taking a strategic and proactive approach to the management of human resources. If this is done, these changes, which may initially be perceived as threats, can be neutralized, minimized, or even turned into advantages that could become a valuable competitive edge for the organization.

Organizations have many challenges confronting them. One of the most critical is the effective management of human resources in a period of tumult. This challenge can be met in part with a strategic approach to the management of human resources. This means integrating the planning and management of human resources with the strategy of the business. The purpose of this report is to provide some guidelines on how this can be accomplished.

II Overview of the Study

Origins of the Study

The study had its origins in 1979 when a number of senior human resource executives, who were members of the Council of Personnel Executives of The Conference Board of Canada, wanted to explore the relationship between business planning and human resource planning. These ten individuals, all of whom had overall corporate human resource responsibility in their respective organizations, believed the various techniques available for the management of human resources were fairly well developed. This included techniques to assist with manpower planning, performance reviewing, salary administration, succession planning, etc. They concluded, however, that there was a gap in knowledge at the strategic level, specifically dealing with the linkages between long-term human resource planning and overall strategic planning and management.

As a first step in exploring this relationship, the participants, with assistance from The Conference Board of Canada, developed a set of conditions or principles that were considered important in integrating human resource planning with strategic planning. If these principles were met, it was believed an organization would be in a better position to deal with the management of human resources from a strategic perspective. The next step was to test the principles among the ten organizations. During 1980, several meetings were held where participants explained to one another how their organization managed the link between human resource and business planning. Following these meetings, two further sessions were held to re-examine the original principles. A number were revised and combined, resulting in the seven principles described in this report.

As a final part of the study, the seven principles were discussed with the chief executive officers of a number of the organizations involved in the research. The purpose of these meetings was not to confirm or reject the principles but, rather, to learn how these individuals viewed the role of human resources in their organizations, and how it could be linked to business planning. Various observations made at these meetings have been incorporated into the report.

Objectives of the Study

The study has two objectives:

- To provide a framework that can be used by organizations to enhance organizational effectiveness through the integration of human resource with overall strategic planning and management.

- To provide a description and analysis of how a number of organizations manage these linkages.

The framework provided in this report focuses on a set of principles that need to exist in any organization in order to facilitate the proper environment for human resource management. While the seven principles are based on the experiences of a small number of organizations, they are presented as underlying or universal principles that can be adapted to other organizations.

The study aims to encourage discussion within organizations about the validity of the principles; it also hopes to provide a basis for discerning whether or not the principles are being utilized effectively. This assessment will be somewhat subjective, as no specific quantitative measures to determine effectiveness can be provided. The description of the principles, coupled with the examples, will, it is hoped, provide a basis for exploring current performance and examining ways of improving the management of human resources from a strategic perspective.

Who Will Use the Study?

The study is aimed at the overall management of the organization and the contribution of human resources to the total business planning and management process. It is line managers who have primary responsibility for the management of the organization's human resources. It is important that they, particularly senior line managers, understand the relationship between business planning and the management of human resources, and ensure that this understanding is fostered throughout the organization. The study is also directed to managers of the human resource function, whose role is to provide leadership for the organization in terms of identifying trends and assisting in charting the future direction of the business as well as to give advice and assistance to all parts of the organization in human resource management. The report should be useful to human resource functional managers because it provides a framework for thinking about their role. It is also hoped that those who are either teaching or conducting research in human resources will find the study useful.

Although the study is based on the experiences of private sector organizations, the principles can also be applied, in large part, to public sector organizations. Indeed, in discussions of the study's findings with a variety of executive groups in public sector organizations at both the federal and provincial levels of government, it was concluded that the principles were highly applicable and that the similarities of practice were far greater than the differences. As well, the ten organizations that took part in the research are all large organizations. It was not possible therefore to test the principles on smaller organizations, including the faster growing more entrepreneurial-oriented organizations. Again it is felt that the principles would apply in a general sense, although their specific application may vary.

What the Study Does Not Deal with

The study is not a survey of human resource practices in a large number of organizations. It provides the perspectives of a limited number of Canadian organizations from a diverse number of industries. As such, it has been written with the aim of sharing experiences and testing ideas rather than providing definitive answers in a broad range of human resource matters (if that were, in fact, possible).

Second, the study does not attempt to establish a relationship between the effectiveness with which human resource planning is integrated into the organization *and* the success or failure of a business, the latter being far more complex than simple relationships between one set of variables and a particular outcome. As an organization reaches a stage of optimal integration of human resource and business planning, it is more likely to take advantage of opportunities that come its way than if the state of integration was minimal. To go any further in terms of cause and effect would be misleading and counterproductive.

Third, none of the participants in the study would suggest that their organizations are coping in all seven areas to an optimal degree. Rather, each felt they were following a number of the principles effectively, and were striving to improve their performance in others. Collectively, the ten organizations characterize desirable practice in an overall sense.

The seven principles outlined in this report are not intended to be used a checklist or as a framework that in practice can or should be followed in a sequential order. Organizations tend to deal with problems and react to opportunities, and do not usually follow a sequence of principles such as that presented in this report. Specific principles will be relevant at particular points in time. Opportunities to improve effectiveness in the management of human resources must be grasped when they occur and not shunned because they do not follow a neat pattern.

The study contains examples of practice taken from the participating organizations in order to illustrate the study's principles. During the course of the research, some of these practices changed and more are likely to be developed by the time this study is published. Thus, the examples throughout the report should be viewed as providing insight into the practices of a number of organizations at a given time as opposed to a documentation of "best practice."

Finally, the study covers a wide variety of areas in the management of human resources. As such, it was necessary to deal with many of the areas in a cursory fashion. The study's contribution, it is felt, is in providing an overview of various aspects of the relationship between human resource and strategic planning. More detailed analyses of specific areas can be obtained from other sources. Also, future research may well explore some of these areas in detail.

The Principles

The aim of this study is to provide a number of underlying or universal principles that relate to the effective integration of human resources with strategic planning and management. Although the principles are presented in general terms, discussion and examples provided in each chapter expand upon their intent and meaning. This elaboration should enable readers to make comparisons with their own organization's practices. Each principle should be read starting with the following preamble.

Effective human resource management, in the context of overall business planning and management, is facilitated to the extent that. . .

1. there is an overall corporate purpose and that the human resource dimensions of that purpose are evident.

2. a process of developing strategy within the organization exists and is understood, and that there is explicit consideration of human resource dimensions.

3. effective linkages exist on a continuing basis to ensure the integration of human resource considerations with the organizational decision-making processes.

4. the office of the chief executive officer provides the climate for integrating human resource considerations to the needs of the business.

5. the organization at all levels establishes responsibility and accountability for human resource management.

6. initiatives in the management of human resources are relevant to the needs of the business.

7. it includes the responsibility to identify and interact in the social, political, technological and economic environments in which the organization is and will be doing business.

Underlying Themes

The study is based on four themes, which flow throughout various chapters:

- The study has a *general management focus* and examines the role played by *all* managers in the management of human resources.

- The organization's *orientation* or its attitude towards its human resources is fundamental, and in many ways is more important than the techniques (systems, programs, etc.) used in the management of these resources. Orientation refers to the values and beliefs about people and characterizes the way an organization thinks and behaves with respect to its human resources. It is demonstrated in many ways (action, words) and is consistent and constant.

- Human resource management is a *line manager's responsibility*. Line managers at all levels of the organization have the primary responsibility in this area.

- The role of managers of the human resource function is to *meet the needs of the business*. It is important that these managers be well versed in the needs of the business.

Examples will be given and references will be made to these underlying themes throughout the report.

The Organizations Involved in the Study

The ten organizations that participated in the study were identified in the foreword to this report. They represent a cross section of Canadian business from the manufacturing and service sectors, from Canadian-owned to foreign-owned multinationals, from capital-intensive to labour-intensive firms, and from widely diversified to single industry business organizations.

The examples used throughout the report will not be identified as to the organization from which they were taken. Each organization has been assigned a number (from one to ten), which is shown on the exhibits and appendices, so that examples taken from the same organization can be followed throughout the report.

III Corporate Purpose

The corporate purpose deals with the organization's philosophy about its world. It is here that management describes its value system. The purpose sets the tone for the corporate culture, which underlines all planning including human resource planning.

CEO of a Canadian multinational corporation

This quotation captures the essence of the first of the seven principles of this study. It deals with corporate purpose and the role it plays in the effective integration of human resources with strategic planning and management. The principle is stated below, followed by an examination of the role of corporate purpose and its use in organizations, including a number of examples. Some important dimensions of the principle, the use of written expressions of purpose, and the human resources component of statements of purpose are also discussed. Finally, the need for developing statements of corporate purpose is assessed.

Principle 1

> Effective human resource management, in the context of overall business planning and management, is facilitated to the extent that *there is an overall understood corporate purpose and that the human resource dimensions of that purpose are evident.*

The term *corporate purpose* referred to in this study denotes the expression of the basic principles or values and beliefs that guide the business operations of a particular organization. A variety of terms are used in practice and are referred to interchangeably in this study. These include corporate philosophy and corporate principles. In the words of one of the participants:

Whatever terms are used in a particular organization, they have to provide a framework for managing the business. They have to be sufficiently broad and all encompassing to permit the development of more specific policies and practices throughout the organization.

It is important that the corporate purpose establish a clear expression of the values and beliefs of the organization. These values and beliefs state what the organization believes to be true about its resources and its principles of operation. It expresses the organization's commitment to these resources and operating principles. Resources could be financial, technological and human, while operating principles could refer to services, profits, safety, codes of behaviour, products, social responsibility, etc.

The Role of Organizational Purpose

Those who participated in the study felt that a clear expression of corporate purpose was a necessary condition in order that effective integration between strategic and human resource planning take place. It was considered essential that there be a clear understanding, particularly among senior executives, of the values and beliefs concerning the organization and its resources. One individual stated:

> The statement of corporate purpose in and of itself is not the important consideration. If the statement is to be useful it must be translated into corporate policies and, more importantly, into practice. It has to be an important part of thinking about the running of the business. The statement of purpose is but the starting point.

Another said:

> The reason for articulating statements of philosophy or purpose is to help focus on the organizational culture or values. It is to define various principles of managing the organization, which are important in guiding the behaviour of others.

What would compel an organization to decide that it was desirable or necessary to define or redefine its organizational purpose? Some reasons are implicit in the quotations above. Others will be addressed later in this chapter.

The State of Practice

An assessment of the degree to which the first principle is being met in a particular organization is, at best, subjective. There are no quantitative measures that can be utilized since the assessment is drawn mainly from perceptions. If these perceptions are shared by others in the organization, tentative conclusions can be reached. As a starting point in this assessment, it is natural to look at published statements of corporate purpose. The following summarizes the situation in the ten organizations involved in the study:

- Four had written statements of corporate philosophy or principles that existed in one document.

- Five lacked such statements in a single document but had a number of statements, which appeared in various organizational policy documents.

- One organization had, by design, no written documentation of company philosophy, but believed it was following the first principle tacitly.

There is thus no clear pattern of practice among the ten organizations with respect to documentation. However, documentation is but a starting point. It is important to understand and carry out the principles whether written or unwritten. One chief executive officer expressed the following view:

> If the senior executive group can satisfy itself that there is a set of guiding principles, and that they are understood and practised, then whether or not they are in one statement, a variety of statements, or no statements is secondary.

Two Examples

Examples from two of the participating organizations that contained statements of corporate purpose in one document are shown in Appendix A. In both cases, extensive involvement of senior executives was an integral part of the formulation of the statements. The resulting documents were then distributed widely both within and outside the organization. In the case of Organization 5, the merger of two quite different organizations (in terms of management philosophy and principles of operation) necessitated the development of a clear statement of principles that would guide the operation of the new organization. In Organization 2, several problems, which emerged at approximately the same time, led the chief executive officer to conclude that it would be useful to develop a statement of corporate philosophy. (This case will be described in more detail later in the chapter.) The two examples presented in Appendix A are meant to be illustrative and not necessarily the "best practice." The real test of the study's first principle is whether the corporate philosophy is understood and practised rather than how it is presented on paper.

Examining the Principle

At this point it is useful to examine a number of dimensions of the principle, which emerged from discussions among the participants.

- *Orientation* about corporate purpose is more important than *technique*, for there must be an interest in and concern for organizational values and beliefs. Orientation, or corporate attitudes, are demonstrated in many ways in the actions of individuals, and become a way of thinking in the organization. The specific techniques used to document the corporate purpose are secondary and will relate to the needs and interests of each organization.

- The *existence* of an overall purpose is an essential aspect of the principle. Regardless of whether the purpose is documented or not, it must exist in the minds and actions of members of the organization.

- The *process of developing* the statement of purpose is important and that those implementing the corporate purpose (at least at the senior levels of the organization) must also be involved in its development.

- The values and beliefs about *human resources* (as well as other resources such as financial, technical, etc.) should be articulated in the corporate purpose. This point will be examined later in the chapter.

- It is essential that the expression of purpose be *understood* not only by the senior management of the organization but also by a large segment of employees.

- *Congruence* between purpose and behaviour is vital. As one participant said:

    If the purpose accurately reflects the orientation of the business, and if there is congruence between the written word and the organizational culture, then the result will be positive. Where there is incongruity — when we are preaching something in the written word that we are not living up to — then we are better off without a written document because it will be dysfunctional.

- Purpose may *change* over time. There should be a method to revise the stated corporate purpose as conditions warrant.

Written Expressions of Purpose

The need to have a written corporate philosophy was examined in some depth by the study's participants. Although not essential, it was considered highly desirable to have the expression of the purpose in writing. This ensures a better understanding of corporate purpose not only for those drafting the statement but also for all other individuals in the organization. The writing and dissemination of corporate philosophy should be tailored to the situation and the culture of the organization. One participant stated:

    Where, for example, you have a family business (even a large one) it may not be desirable to put the philosophy in writing. As well, where there is a very charismatic leader, it may not be useful or desirable because the orientation regarding philosophy is a living and well communicated process.

    On the other hand, where there is a multi-faceted organization with significant delegation, and where people tend to become somewhat isolated in their own area, it is desirable to express the purpose in writing.

    Also, one must guard against a written statement becoming a barrier or a constraint. The vision of senior management people as well as others in the organization could be limited as a result.

The same participant commented that although his organization's philosophy about human resources was unwritten he felt there would be wide agreement in the organization, at least at the senior levels, on the elements of this philosophy. These elements were described as follows:

> There are three elements to our human resource philosophy. First, the company does not own its employees. They belong to the family (self) as much as to the job they do. Second, employees whose lives are better integrated in terms of self, community and job will be better employees. This integration will lead to a more realistic representation of their environment, a better understanding of the needs of our customers and, a better basis in obtaining ongoing feedback on the company from the community. Third, individual employees are expected to play an active part in planning their own careers and are provided with the specific tools to do so by the company.

Another comment on this topic, with respect to large multi-faceted organizations, is instructive:

> From a practical point of view, how do you transmit corporate philosophy throughout an organization of some 60,000 people if it is not in writing? I feel it is important for it to be in writing, although you do not refer to it daily. If it is written there is a reference, which can be consulted when need be.

Human Resource Component

A part of Principle 1 states that integration of human resources and business planning is facilitated to the extent that the *human resource dimensions* of the organization's purpose are clear. Such dimensions articulate the organization's values relating to people and could include beliefs about the following: open communication, developmental responsibilities, rewards for performance, equal opportunity, employee input into decision making, etc. The statements of corporate purpose for the two organizations, used as examples earlier in the chapter, included sections that dealt specifically with human resources. The human resource component from the first example (Organization 5) is presented in its entirety in Appendix B.

A review of the statements in Appendix B leads to an understanding of that organization's philosophy of management. The statements also provide a reference point for the development of corporate policies and practices in the human resources area. For example, one statement (number 7) describes a decentralized approach to decision making. This will have an impact on how the organization deals with the division of responsibility between corporate and divisional personnel activities.[1] The human resource component of the Statement of Corporate Purpose for the second organization is shown in Appendix A. It is found in the Statement of Corporate Objectives, specifically under item (2.); and in the Statement of Corporate Policies, item (1.), (a) to (g).

---
[1]   This topic is examined in Chapter V.

A Final Example

Another of the organizations involved in the study developed a statement of corporate philosophy as part of a document used internally to describe the organization's management system. The document is designed to assist new managers in familiarizing themselves with the organization's management style and is also referred to periodically by senior management to assess the continued practice and relevance of the statement of purpose. The introduction of this statement is presented in Appendix C. This expression of corporate philosophy was prepared by the chief executive officer as a way of outlining his philosophy of management. The philosophy is based on the belief that people must be trusted and will act in a responsible manner and stresses the importance of trust, mutual respect, objectivity and open communication. This philosophy is the underpinning of the company's management concept. This same organization recently published a document entitled *A Statement of Management Philosophy* for all employees, which contains elements of the organization's management system. This document is also shown in Appendix C in its entirety.

Organizational Purpose as a Way of Managing

The three examples presented in this chapter portray different approaches to specifying corporate purpose. Further, five of the ten organizations had aspects of corporate purpose statements in various sources. One had no written reference to corporate purpose. Notwithstanding the spectrum of approaches, the existence of a clearly understood overall purpose for the organization was felt to be a necessary condition for the effective integration of human resource management with overall business planning and management. Written statements of corporate purpose made it easier to meet the condition.

The test of the principle, however, is not in the statement of purpose, but in its application. The values and benefits expressed in the statement must be an integral part of the decision making processes of the business. The following comment illustrates this point:

> What is so important is the cultural system of the organization wherein the values and beliefs about the organization are continually reinforced, mostly by examples, in an organized and systematic way. It does not take people long to learn about the values and culture of the organization and about many things including its human resources. People see values in behaviour.

> The test of organizational purpose is in the execution, and the burden of this is on every manager in the organization.

Assessing Need

There is nothing particularly new about Principle 1. It is a principle most would agree has merit. Because statements of corporate purpose are so general, it could be argued that they are of limited use. Why then would an organization want to reassess its purpose, probably at the expenditure of significant time? Not all organizations would think it was necessary to define or redefine the corporate purpose. Some would feel that it would not be a high priority need; others would feel satisfied with their performance in this area. Since much of an organization's behaviour is in response to needs usually initiated by a problem, energy devoted to examining corporate purpose is likely to be initiated by a need. Further, the need has to be important enough for someone to want to do something about it. Thus, an organization would undertake to reconsider its purpose because:

- The relevance of the current philosophy in the ever-changing environment is felt to be inadequate.

- There is an incongruence between corporate purpose and organizational behaviour.

- Someone in a position of influence wants it to happen.

Such was the case with one of the organizations described earlier in this chapter. The final section of this chapter describes the process of redefining corporate purpose, which took place in Organization 2 in 1977 and 1978.

In this company, two needs converged at approximately the same time. One need came from the external environment. Questions were asked from a variety of sources outside the organization about its mission and about its stance on topics such as social responsibility and corporate codes of conduct. There had been several of these questions raised at recent shareholders' meetings. At approximately the same time there was an increased feeling along similar lines from inside the organization. The organization had grown significantly, and there was an increasing number of managers coming up through the ranks who had not been with the company very long and who were not thoroughly familiar with the organization's beliefs and principles. Up to this point, there was no single document to describe these principles because the need had not been envisaged.

Convergence of these two needs led the chairman and chief executive officer to conclude that it was important to specify, in writing, a statement of the organization's purpose. Work began in early 1977 and was finalized and approved by the board of directors in mid-1978. During this time, some 200 senior managers from around the world were involved in shaping the statement. The statement, which is presented in Appendix A, went through some 45 drafts before it was presented to the board. It was then subjected to further review before finally being approved. It should be noted that the document, which was sent to all employees, shareholders and others, was but the start of a process that led to a reassessment of the strategic direction of the organization.[2] The document was very well received by employees around the world. When the process of preparing the written document was completed, it was felt that a good sense of the organization's purpose had been developed by the 200 senior executives of the corporation. Much remained to be done. The real test would be how the philosophy would manifest itself in organizational behaviour. Finally, the six senior executives agreed to a periodic critique of how the organization was measuring up to its stated corporate philosophy. Also, they encouraged managers to raise questions when the company's actions were in apparent conflict with its philosophy.

One of the executives stated:

> For us, a number of things came together to make our process happen. I am not certain it would have taken place without these needs coming to bear on us at one point in time. One can have a conceptual framework, but it must fit into what is happening in the company and what the needs and priorities are.

A senior executive officer of this organization (and the chief executive of its largest subsidiary) described his observations on the process some two years after the formal phase of the process had been completed. These observations are summarized in Appendix D.

Conclusion

The need for a clearly understood corporate purpose is usually accepted without question. This chapter suggests that it may prove useful to assess the degree to which an organization's philosophy is actually understood by senior managers and others, for a clearly understood purpose is essential to the effective integration of human resource planning with overall business planning.

---

[2] Strategy formulation is the subject of the next chapter.

IV   The Strategic Planning Process

> In the 1980s, the critical factor limiting our growth potential will not be capital or technology but the ability to develop and acquire human resources.
>
> CEO of a large resource-based company

> No major appropriation request will be approved by the board of directors unless there is a thorough analysis of the human resource needs whether they be managerial, technical or production.
>
> CEO of a Canadian-based manufacturing company

> In our company, we are looking at three scenarios for 1985. The one limiting factor in all three scenarios is people.
>
> CEO of a high-technology company

As these three quotations testify, it is essential that organizations take a strategic approach to managing human resources because these resources play as important a role in planning as do capital or physical resources. This led to the framing of the second principle of the study, which deals with the strategic planning process, and its human resource dimensions.

The first section of the chapter describes briefly the evolution of human resource planning in organizations, followed by a description of the second principle including definition of terms. The chapter concludes with an examination of a number of case studies taken from the participating organizations on how human resource planning is integrated with the strategic planning process.

Human Resources and Corporate Strategy — An Evolution

The explicit consideration of human resources as a *critical factor* in the strategic planning process is a relatively recent phenomenon. This is not to say that human resource considerations were not taken into account in the planning context in the past. It does suggest, however, that human resource considerations have tended to be after-the-fact or secondary in nature. In other words, human resource planning has not been, and is still not in many cases, *systematically* integrated with strategic planning in a *consistent and disciplined* manner. One of the participants stated:

> Strategic planning in many organizations over the past ten years has been undergoing evolutionary change and has gone through a number of phases. Initially, planning took place in a period of relatively little change in the social, political and economic environments. In the next phase,

planning took place in a period of change in these environments, but that the change was predictable. The current phase is a period where the environment is definitely changing and in many instances these changes are unpredictable. Strategic planning must make an effort to come to grips with the non-predictability of these environments, perhaps through the more effective use of planning-type scenarios.

Only during the past five years or so have organizations begun to include the human resource factor in their strategic thinking and it is still at an early stage of development.

There are other reasons why long-range human resource planning, in the context of strategic planning, became important. Strategic planning has been, and generally is, market driven, which demands an assessment of customers, competitors, margins, costs, etc., with, in most cases, the implicit assumption that the "people" needs can always be met within a fairly short time horizon. As indicated earlier, a number of organizations are realizing that human resources have become a limiting factor, but more important, human resource *management* is increasingly being seen as an essential competitive tool. This was described as follows:

The focus on strategic thinking opposite employee relations is new for our system world-wide. It is new because we now realize that productivity cannot be achieved by technology alone and that people are the mortar. Also, in the future, we will be dealing with the management of scarcity, and one of these scarcities is people. Technology, in our business, is far ahead of our capabilities to use it because of human resource limitations.

These changes have led to a shift in the importance of the employee relations activity. It is critical that employee relations respond to this shifting emphasis and play a leadership role.

The role of human resources in the strategic planning process continues to evolve due to an increasing number of human resource functional executives who are viewing their role in a different light. Traditional personnel specialists have viewed their role as being reactive, dealing primarily with the maintenance and protection of employee relations systems. In too many instances, innovations in human resources were designed to meet the needs of the specialists instead of the business. The credibility and relevance of the human resource function as an important component of the business were questioned.

Increasingly, human resource executives are viewing their role as one of meeting the business needs of their organizations. This has led to a constructive reassessment of the role of the employee relations function and its future directions. In the words of one participant:

It is essential that we understand the needs of the business we are serving and become actively involved in assisting to meet — and thus influence — the outcome of the business.

The realization that human resource considerations can hinder growth, and may also lead to a change in corporate strategy, has led to the need for a more effective way of linking human resource planning with strategic planning. In the future, this linkage will be managed in a more disciplined and systematic manner, particularly for larger organizations. This is a challenge for both senior line executives and human resource professionals. The examples in the latter part of this chapter are intended to provide illustrations of how a number of organizations manage this linkage.

Principle 2

> Effective human resource management, in the context of overall business planning and management, is facilitated to the extent that *a process of developing strategy within the organization exists and is understood, and that there is explicit consideration of human resource dimensions.*

This principle has two aspects. First, that the process for developing strategy *exists* and is *understood*, and second, that there is *explicit consideration* of the human resource dimensions. If the first aspect does not exist, the second cannot take place.

Defining Strategy

It is necessary to define the terms strategic and operational planning for the purposes of this study. *Strategic planning* deals with the long-term direction of the organization while *operational planning* deals with the short term. The time frame for strategic planning will vary depending on the organization and could be anywhere from five to twenty-five years. Said one participant:

> Operational planning is the projection of today forward while strategic planning is the painting of a scenario for the future and coming back from that future.

Another commented:

> Strategic decisions consist of commitments that, when put into operation, are either irreversible or reversible at great cost.

Orientation versus Technique

As stated in Chapter II, an organization's orientation towards human resources is more important than the techniques it uses to manage those resources. In this present chapter, *orientation* means that the strategic planning process is clearly seen as important and is demonstrated by the behaviour of the senior executive group. Specific techniques for carrying out the planning process will vary and will relate to a number of factors including organizational size and structure, as well as the nature of the industry or industries in which the firm operates. It is also important that the link between human resource planning and strategic planning be viewed as important. Again, how this takes place will relate to the needs of the organization.

Examining the Principle

The first part of Principle 2 states that effective integration can only take place if a process of developing strategy within the organization *exists* and is *understood*. The participants in the study agreed that this part of the principle was not only an underlying condition for effective integration, it was absolutely necessary for all modern organizations. Only a subjective assessment can be made to judge whether this condition is being met. Some standards or benchmarks are necessary, which is the reason for the examples that are presented later in this chapter. In general, an assessment has to be based largely on the quality of the strategic plan that is generated and to some extent on the success in attaining the plan.

In spite of the great diversity of practice among the ten organizations taking part in the study, the participants felt their organizations met this condition to a high degree — there was already a process in place doing an effective job at generating strategies. However, it was agreed there was room for improvement.

The second part of this principle states that there must be *explicit consideration* of the organization's human resources in the strategic plan. One participant said:

> It is critical that human resources be part of management thinking in the strategic planning process. This is the orientation; the technique will vary.

In many large organizations the senior human resource executive will be involved in the strategic planning process. It is important that this involvement be active and result in an ongoing assessment of the impact on human resources of various strategic thrusts. It should be noted that the absence of the senior human resource executive in the strategic formulation process cannot be construed to indicate that human resources are not being given explicit consideration. In such cases, it is incumbent on other senior executives to ensure that this take place.

Some Examples of Practice

Strategic planning and the relationship between strategic planning and human resource planning is extremely complex. The case examples, presented below provide some idea of the degree to which the relationship is managed in a number of organizations. It is important to note that these cases are not complete descriptions of strategic planning processes; rather they are highly summarized descriptions that highlight the integration of human resources with strategic planning. Some of the case examples illustrate the strategic planning *process*, while others focus on the *content* of the plans.

Example 1   Organization 2

This organization developed its future strategy following the completion of a major project of defining its purpose and principles of operation as described in Chapter III. In part, the process of reassessing the corporate purpose led to the realization that the strategic shape of the organization also had to be re-examined. The strategic plan was developed by the management committee of the corporation, which consisted of the chairman and chief executive officer, the president, the vice chairman, three regional executive vice presidents, the chief financial officer, and the corporate planner. The process resulted in a document that outlined the strategic shape for the corporation for the next ten to fifteen years. This plan examined ten different areas:

- General planning
- Management process and corporate structure
- Personnel
- Raw materials
- Semi-fabricating
- Finished products
- Trading
- Technology and engineering
- Finance
- Public affairs

The section on personnel, which was viewed as an important part of the overall management strategy, is examined below.

Human Resource Dimensions

The document describing the strategic shape of the organization provided broad brush statements of strategic directions and priorities for each of the ten areas identified above. These strategic directions for personnel are presented in Exhibit I.

Describing the process of defining purpose, objectives and policies and the strategic shape document, the chief executive officer of this organization noted the following:

Throughout the process of developing the overall strategy, a climate was being set, attitudes were redirected, and action plans supporting strategic plans in the area of human resources were being developed. Subsequent strategic plans coming in from the field were heavily influenced by the "shape" document and contained, to a lesser or greater degree, human resource strategy.

The senior human resource executive of this organization provided some background information on the meaning of the five items in Exhibit 1. These comments are contained in Appendix E. Human resource dimensions in the strategic shape document provided a focal point for the development of specific objectives for human resources at the corporate, group, and divisional levels. These objectives will be examined in subsequent chapters.

Example 2 — Organization 3

The second example is from a large multi-industry manufacturing company, which follows a disciplined strategic planning process involving all levels of management and all functional disciplines. A strategic plan is developed for each of the businesses as well as for the corporation as a whole. The process of developing

---

Exhibit 1

Corporate Strategic Human Resource Guidelines — Organization 2

1. The company will have a management group composed of both managers and staff specialists who are well balanced in professional skills, international outlook, and experience. This will require a commitment from all levels of management for the training, development and deployment of present and future members of this group, and will require taking into account the employees' needs and aspirations as well as the company's needs.

2. All subsidiary companies will have programs to improve the quality of working relationships with all employees in order to achieve both recognition of mutual interdependence and high personal commitment.

3. Each company manufacturing unit will have a health and safety program.

4. Alterations or reductions in employment will be made in such a way as to minimize adverse effects on employees.

5. Each manager in the company will recognize that his accountability involves sharing openly the plans and relevant information concerning all the resources entrusted to their stewardship with his superior and others in the group.

---

strategy for a business is examined first, followed by an examina
tion of the corporate approach.

The strategic plan for each business is reviewed annually.
Strategic time horizons will vary from five to fifteen years, depending on the business. The first year of the strategic planning
cycle is the operating or budget year. The planning process is por-

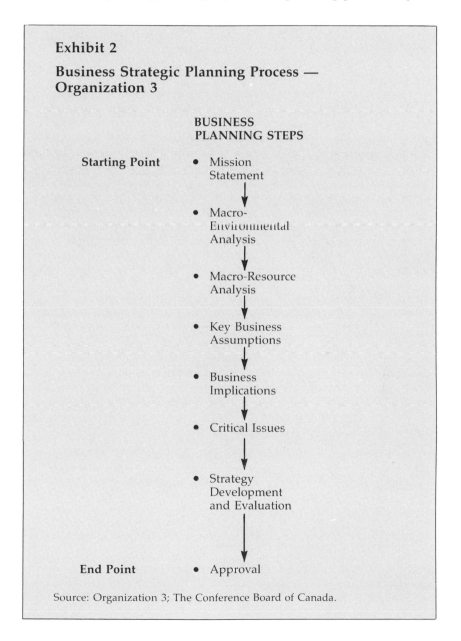

Exhibit 2

**Business Strategic Planning Process —
Organization 3**

BUSINESS
PLANNING STEPS

Starting Point • Mission
                  Statement

                • Macro-
                  Environmental
                  Analysis

                • Macro-Resource
                  Analysis

                • Key Business
                  Assumptions

                • Business
                  Implications

                • Critical Issues

                • Strategy
                  Development
                  and Evaluation

End Point   • Approval

Source: Organization 3; The Conference Board of Canada.

trayed in Exhibit 2, starting with a statement outlining the mission of the business. This is combined with the results of a number of analyses made of the environment that identify the threats and opportunities for the business (macro-environmental analysis), and of the available resources (macro-resource analysis) that identify company strengths and weaknesses, and of certain basic assumptions about the future (key business assumptions). These analyses lead to the determination of critical issues facing the business, i.e., those that stand in the way of the company achieving its goals. At this point, one or more strategic thrusts are generally drafted, i.e., those key strategies on which the success or failure of the strategic plan hinges.

These strategic thrusts then pass through a number of functional (engineering, employee relations) evaluations or screens to identify what implications each have for each of the business functions. In this way, the critical functional issues, as well as the resource requirements and costs are determined. For example, in the human resource function, the following are some of the aspects that are examined when reviewing a proposed business thrust: manpower requirements, union-employee implications, compensation, occupational health and safety, and organizational change. The screening process is virtually a functional version of the strategic planning process. It can, and does, bring forth legal, technical, financial, employee or other issues, which will result in modification to the basic strategies or even to the business objectives.

The overall planning process is therefore reiterated until the business strategies have been shaped sufficiently to ensure that all of the critical issues are addressed and that management is satisfied that all objectives can be met. The relationship between strategic planning and human resource planning for the corporation is diagrammatically depicted in Appendix F. It shows the steps involved in the development of corporate strategies and the relationship between corporate and business unit planning as well as corporate and business unit employee relations planning.

The Human Resource Component

In this company, human resource considerations are an essential part of the overall strategy for the business. Exhibit 3 expands on Exhibit 2 and depicts the manner in which human resources have an impact on the strategic planning process for the business. The senior human resource executive said:

> The human resource contribution to the planning process is focused strictly on supporting business strategies.

As the business unit goes through the steps in developing its strategic plan (the left side of Exhibit 3) the human resource function considers human resource dimensions of the business's strategy (the right side of Exhibit 3). This starts with a statement of the business thrust and proceeds through an analysis of the overall environment of the business in terms of human resources and an assessment of the human resources of the business (skill mix, demographics of the work force, etc.). It ends with an assessment of human resource strategies and an evaluation for its inclusion in the

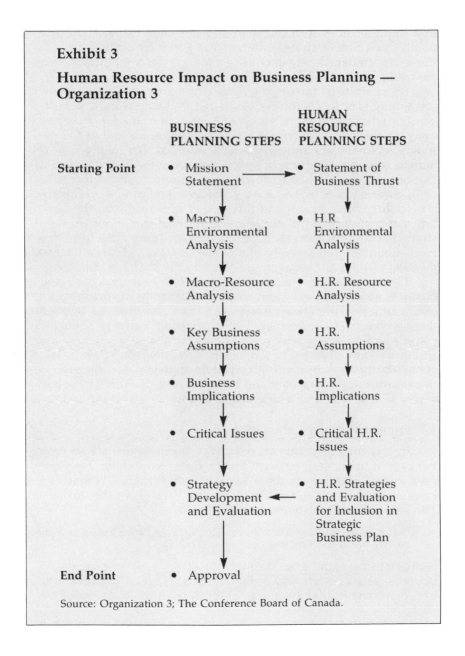

Exhibit 3

Human Resource Impact on Business Planning — Organization 3

	BUSINESS PLANNING STEPS	HUMAN RESOURCE PLANNING STEPS
Starting Point	• Mission Statement ———→	• Statement of Business Thrust
	• Macro-Environmental Analysis	• H.R. Environmental Analysis
	• Macro-Resource Analysis	• H.R. Resource Analysis
	• Key Business Assumptions	• H.R. Assumptions
	• Business Implications	• H.R. Implications
	• Critical Issues	• Critical H.R. Issues
	• Strategy Development ←——— and Evaluation	• H.R. Strategies and Evaluation for Inclusion in Strategic Business Plan
End Point	• Approval	

Source: Organization 3; The Conference Board of Canada.

strategic plan of the business unit. In summing up the process, the senior human resource executive commented:

> If critical issues are identified, they have to be addressed in the strategy and be supported by plans and they have to be tied back to the overall strategy of the business.

Appendix F shows how human resource considerations have an impact on the corporate strategic plan and how the same process takes place at the departmental or business unit level.

Example 3 — Organization 7

The next example is from a Canadian-based high technology company. The strategic objectives of the corporation are developed by the Policy Committee, comprising the chief executive officer and the executive vice presidents, and is communicated to subsidiary companies both in formal documents and through meetings between the chief executive officer of the corporation and the chief executive officer of the subsidiary.

The strategic planning process (five-year plan) is conducted annually by each business unit (division). The resulting business plan is subjected to review by the Policy Committee and the subsidiary's executive management. After consolidation of divisional plans into subsidiary business plans, the subsidiary plan is in turn subjected to critical review by corporate executive management and their staff. Major milestones of the process are shown in Exhibit 4.

Business plans of subsidiary companies are market driven, but integrate all functional aspects of the business, including human resources

---

Exhibit 4

Strategic and Business Planning Cycle — Organization 8

MILESTONE	COMPLETION
Procedural Guidelines	Mid-January
Corporate Strategy and Objectives	End-January
Divisional Plans (Tentative) Released	Early May
Group/Divisional Plan Reviewed	Mid-May
Subsidiary Plans Released	End-May
Corporate Summary of Subsidiary Plans	Mid-June
Policy Committee Review and Approval	Late-June

The Human Resource Component

This company has developed a human resource business planning cycle that results in a human resource component in the overall corporate strategic plan and a human resource component for each of the subsidiaries' five-year business plans. The planning cycle will be described in some detail in Chapter VIII. In summary the process is as follows:

- The corporate human resource function generates a list of corporate-wide human resource issues and concerns for the planning horizon (five years). This is based in part on the predetermined statement of corporate strategy and objectives.

- This list is given to the human resource executive at the subsidiary level who uses the information as partial input to the development of the subsidiary's five-year business plan. The subsidiary's human resource executive is highly involved with his chief executive officer and other executives of the subsidiary in the development of their business plan.

- When completed, the human resource component of the business plans for all subsidiaries is reviewed by the corporate human resources group for similarities and differences.

- Using the original list of corporate-wide issues and concerns and the subsidiary's plan, the corporate human resource function develops the human resource component of the corporate strategic plan for the next five years.

Exhibit 5 summarizes the nine major strategic thrusts for the corporation over the next five years, which are supported by more detailed quantitative information.

Example 4 — Organization 10

This final example provides a slightly different perspective on the human resource portion of a strategic plan. The 1980 corporate strategic plan for this organization consisted of a section on human resources, which included an environmental analysis and a number of key planning assumptions and implications that flowed from the analysis. Portions of this information are shown in Appendix G.

Conclusion

Strategic planning is a complex subject. The purpose of this chapter has not been to discuss this topic in depth but rather to make the point that human resource considerations must be systematically integrated with the strategic planning process. The examples presented were selected to bring out different aspects of the linkage between human resource and strategic planning, albeit in a highly summarized fashion. The *process* of strategic planning

Exhibit 5

Corporate Strategic Plan — Human Resource Component — Organization 7

AREA	GOALS	RANK[1]	PRIOR- ITIES
Human Resource Requirements	Adequate supply of well trained executives and managers	A	1
	Identification and effective development of employees		
	Optimize retention		
Productivity	Institutionalize productivity improvement program for technical and scientific personnel	A	2
Human Resource Information System	Develop and install a personnel information system	A	3
Planning for Future Needs	Increase involvement in acquisition and divestiture planning	A	4
Responsibilities and Authority	Define and communicate functional responsibilities and authority	A	5
Financing Benefit Programs	Reduce costs and risks	A	6
Employee Relations	Improve employee understanding and acceptance of company's objectives, opportunities and risks	A	7
Government Intervention	Each subsidiary company to have a proactive pro- gram to deal with government intervention	A	8
Development of Human Resource Function	Implement a plan to increase the professional capability of the human resource function	A	9

[1] The exhibit shows only those strategic thrusts with an "A" or highest ranking. The overall ranking system comprises "A", "B" and "C" ranked thrusts. Within each ranking, the human resource topic areas are placed in order of priority.

was illustrated in the example taken from Organization 2. Other examples were selected to illustrate the *content* of the human resource component of a number of strategic plans. Content varies considerably among organizations with some providing general guidelines while others provide specific objectives.

As was mentioned at the outset of the chapter it is difficult for an organization to determine in a precise manner the degree to which Principle 2 is being followed. The assessment has to be based on overall impressions. A beginning point for this assessment would be a discussion by the senior executive group of responses to the following three questions:

1. Does a process of developing strategy in the organization exist?

2. Is the process understood at all relevant levels of the organization?

3. Is there explicit consideration of the human resource dimension of the plan?

V Organizational Linkages

Chapter III dealt with organizational purpose and discussed the importance of a well understood corporate purpose and its human resource dimensions. The previous chapter dealt with explicit consideration of human resources in the process of strategy formulation. This chapter moves one step further and deals with decision-making processes in the organization and how human resource considerations are integrated with these processes. It examines a variety of processes or linkages including those at the level of the board of directors, the senior executive policy group, and other senior levels of the organization.

Principle 3

> Effective human resource management, in the context of overall business planning and management, is facilitated to the extent that *effective linkages exist on a continuing basis to ensure the integration of human resource considerations with the organizational decision-making processes.*

The word *linkages* describes a variety of organizational approaches that can be used to facilitate the integration of human resource considerations with organizational decision making. This includes the more static aspects of organizational structure and reporting relationships as well as membership on particular decision-making groups. It also refers to the equally important aspect of developing and maintaining effective reporting relationships, and their contribution to organizational performance. Effective use of these linkages will reflect an organization's commitment to the integration of human resources with strategic planning and management.

This principle has two important aspects. First, the *existence* of effective mechanisms to integrate the human resource dimensions of a decision with the organization's decision-making processes are required. It is important that the human resource dimensions of a decision be present. This requires the establishment and management of effective linkages throughout the organization, particularly at senior levels. Second, consideration of the human resource dimension of decisions must be applied on a *continual* and *consistent* basis to the workings of the management of the organization. This must not be occasional, reactive or intermittent.

This chapter deals with the linkages that should exist in an organization to ensure human resource elements are considered in all relevant situations. If these linkages are in place, and are managed effectively, an organization will have a sound foundation for effective human resource management. The following linkages are discussed in this chapter:

- between the management organization and the board of directors,

- at the senior executive level of the organization (i.e., the corporate level),

- between the senior human resource executive and line managers at the corporate level and at the subsidiary or business unit levels,

- between human resource functional managers and line managers throughout the organization,

- between the senior human resource executive and his counterparts in subsidiary organizations.

There are many other linkages that could be considered; however, it is felt that if these mechanisms are in place and managed effectively, others will develop at various levels of the organization.

Board of Directors

It is important that there be effective linkages between the management organization and the board of directors on human resource matters. This linkage could take place in several ways, which need not be mutually exclusive:

- The board as a whole could review and approve major decisions. Here is an example taken from one of the organizations:

  Our board approves our executive planning statement, which is the strategic plan for the organization. This document is approved annually and contains explicit reference to the organization's human resources.

- Regular information presentations to the board could be made on various aspects of human resources including performance of the pension plan, senior executive succession, etc.

- Compensation or human resource committees of the board can play an important role in linking human resources to organizational decision making. These committees are examined in the following section.

Human Resource Committees

The ten organizations involved in the study all had some type of human resource committee. For the most part, the mandate of these committees extends beyond the role of the traditional compensation committee and deals with various major aspects of human resources including senior management succession, major organizational changes, etc. Effective human resource committees of the board of directors were considered by the participants to be an important type of linkage. In the words of one participant:

> We have a very effective personnel committee of the board. The members, all outside directors, are very competent and are a real help. Their role is critical to overall aspects of effective human resource planning. Although not a member of this committee, I work very closely with its members.

The mandates of these committees vary and depend upon a number of factors including the role of the committee as viewed by the chief executive officer. A summarized version of the terms of reference of the management resource and compensation committee of one of the organizations participating in the study is shown in Exhibit 6.

It is important that the human resource committee periodically undertakes an assessment of its effectiveness in carrying out its mandate. As well, membership on the committee should be periodically reviewed with respect to its size and composition. The role played by the senior human resource executive on these com-

---

Exhibit 6

Management Resource and Compensation Committee, Terms of Reference — Organization 2

Summarized Version

- Review of competitive position and internal equity of the salaries of senior officers

- Determination of the total corporate bonus fund and the individual payments to senior members of the fund

- Approval of incremental liabilities to the pension plan

- Review of major bargaining settlements

- Review of the current and future organizational structure of the company

- Review of succession plans for senior executives

mittees varied considerably among organizations that participated in the study. In some cases, he served as secretary and attended all meetings.[1] In other cases, he provided staff support and took part regularly, except when confidential information was discussed. The specific role is not considered as important as is the manner in which the senior human resource executive assists the committee in the effective pursuit of its mandate.[2]

The Senior Executive Level

Proper integration of human resource planning and management will take place where there are effective ways of ensuring human resource input to the senior decision-making processes of the organization. Here again it is the organization's *orientation* that is important. In other words, it is the attitude that exists about human resource input into the executive decision-making processes. If it is believed that the input is critical and must take place, then the specific techniques are not as important. If the proper orientation is not present, then technique becomes more important in fostering the proper orientation. This section deals with a number of different aspects of human resource input into the senior decision-making level, namely:

- the reporting relationship of the senior human resource executive,

- the senior decision-making council of the organization and human resource input,

- other senior executive human resource councils and human resource input.

Reporting Relationship: Senior Human Resource Executive

At first sight, one can conclude that for effective integration between human resource and strategic planning and management, the senior human resource executive must report to the chief executive officer.[3] Further reflection, however, indicates that this need not be the case. Effective integration can and does take place without a direct reporting relationship between the senior human resource executive and the chief executive officer. In this regard, a

---

[1] Masculine gender is used throughout this study in the generic sense only and is intended to include both men and women.

[2] For additional information on human resource committees of the board see Susan Peterson, *Compensation/Human Resource Committees of Boards of Directors*, Executive Bulletin No. 6 (Ottawa: The Conference Board in Canada, 1978).

[3] The term "chief executive officer" is used in a generic sense here and could mean, in particular organizations, any of the following: president, president and chief executive officer, chief executive officer, and chairman and chief executive officer.

sub-principle was developed from the experience of the participants in this study:

> Effective human resource management... is facilitated to the extent that *the executive with primary responsibilities for human resources is in a position to be able to influence the senior decision-making levels of the organization.*

Attaining the necessary *position* can occur in a number of ways including a direct reporting relationship with the chief executive officer, membership on senior executive decision-making councils or other means. In terms of effective integration, the reporting relationship with the chief executive officer cannot be looked at in isolation. Overall decision-making processes at the senior executive level and the involvement of the senior human resource executive in these processes must be examined.

Also important is the effectiveness of the senior human resource executive in these processes and the contribution he makes not only through his functional expertise but also by bringing his overall managerial skills to bear on general management issues. Through his professional expertise and managerial leadership, the senior human resource executive must be able to influence matters of importance.

It is instructive to examine the reporting relationship and other linkages of the ten organizations that participated in the study. This information has been summarized in Exhibit 7 (left column).[4]

With regard to the reporting relationship of the senior human resource executive, Exhibit 7 (left column) provides information on the title of the senior corporate human resource officer and his reporting relationship. Of the ten organizations:

- In six, the senior human resource executive reports directly to the chief executive officer.

- In the other four organizations, the human resource executive reports to an executive vice president.[5]

As mentioned earlier, reporting to the chief executive officer, while important, is not considered to be a necessary condition for ensuring effective human resource input into the senior decision-making processes of the organization. In the words of one participant:

---

[4] The exhibit also describes the most senior management council for each of the organizations (middle column) along with the senior human resource executive's involvement with the council. Also portrayed are examples of other senior management forums concerned with human resource matters (right column).

[5] The subject of an indirect reporting relationship (where the senior human resource executive reports through another senior executive to the chief executive officer) is examined later in this chapter.

Exhibit 7

Human Resource Reporting Relationships and Other Senior Organizational Linkages

Title and Reporting Relationship of Senior Human Resource Executive	The Most Senior Management Council(s) and Human Resource Involvement	Other Senior Management Councils Concerned with Human Resource Matters
Organization 1		
• Vice President, Corporate Development	• The Senior Executive Group	• Senior Staff Planning Committee —
	– 4 members	(Vice Presidents, Corporate
• Reports to a Senior Vice President	– Vice President, Corporate	Development plus the Senior
	Development is not a member	Executive Group) Deals with
	but attends when human re-	succession and organization
	source matters are being	planning
	discussed, or when desired	
		• Human Resource Committee —
		Vice Presidents, Business, Finance,
		Corporate Development and
		General Manager, Human
		Resources
Organization 2		
• Corporate Vice President, Personnel	• Management Committee	• Monthly one-day meetings of the
	– 7 members	Management Committee and the
• Reports to the President/Chief Executive Officer[1]	– Corporate Vice President,	Corporate Vice President,
	Personnel, although not a full-time	Personnel. Agenda deals only with
	member, has an open invitation to	organizational and personnel
	attend meeting whenever he feels	matters
	that the subject under discussion	
	has personnel and organizational	• Quarterly meetings of Executive
	implications. He attends about 30	Vice Presidents and Corporate Vice

per cent of the meetings, which are
held about 5–6 times a month

President, Personnel to discuss problems of senior management
deployment

Organization 3

- Vice President, Corporate Human
  Resources
- Reports to the Chairman of
  the Board/Chief Executive Officer

- CEO Committee
  - 9 members
  - Vice President, Human
    Resources is a member
  - meets 6–8 times per year

- Company Corporate Council
  - consists of executive group (25
    members)
  - Vice President, Human
    Resources a member

Organization 4

- Group Vice President, Human
  Resources
- Reports to the Chairman of the
  Board/Chief Executive Officer

- Executive Committee
  - 5 members
  - Group Vice President, Human
    Resources not a member but
    attends most of the meetings

- Human Resource Planning Group
  - 4 members (Chairman, President,
    Executive Vice President, Finance
    and Administration, and Group
    Vice President, Human
    Resources)
  - regular review of major human
    resource programs

Organization 5

- Vice President, Corporate and
  Employee Relations
- Reports to the Executive Vice
  President

- Corporate Management Committee
  - 10 members
  - Vice President, Corporate and
    Employee Relations is a member
  - meets 6–8 times a year

- Manpower Planning Meetings
  - consists of the President,
    Executive Vice President, Vice
    President, Corporate and
    Employee Relations and heads of
    each of the major business units
  - reviews manpower plans as they
    support strategic and operational
    plans
  - meets annually

Exhibit 7

Human Resource Reporting Relationships and Other Senior Organization Linkages (Continued)

Title and Reporting Relationship of Senior Human Resource Executive	The Most Senior Management Council(s) and Human Resource Involvement	Other Senior Management Councils Concerned with Human Resource Matters
Organization 6		

• Vice President, Administration
 	
• Reports to the President/Chief Executive Officer
	• Executive Committee
	  – 7 members
	  – Vice President, Administration is a member
	  – meets twice weekly (plus unstructured meetings on other 3 days
		• General Management Development Committee
		  – 10 members (chaired by CEO)
		  – reviews executive succession planning and development
		  – meets 4 times a year

Organization 7		

• Vice President, Human Resources
 	
• Reports to the Executive Vice President, Administration
	• Policy Committee
	  – 5 members
	  – Executive Vice President, Administration is a member
	
	• Executive Committee
	  – 10 members
	  – Executive Vice President, Administration is a member
	  – meets monthly. Reviews succession and development for top 125 executives in the company. Vice President, Human Resources attends
		• Human Resource Vice Presidents of Business Units
		  – chaired by Corporate Vice President, Human Resources
		  – meets quarterly

Organization 8

- Vice President, Personnel
- Reports to the Executive Vice President, Administration

- Senior Executive Group
  - 7 members
  - Vice President, Personnel not a member but participates when human resource issues are discussed

Organization 9

- Vice President, Human Resources and Public Affairs
- Reports to the President/Chief Executive Officer

- Corporate Management Staff Committee
  - 11 members — meet 8 times a year
  - Vice President, Human Resources and Public Affairs is a member

Organization 10

- Vice President, Personnel
- Reports to the President/Chief Executive Officer

- Management Committee
  - 4 members
  - Vice President, Personnel not a member

- Management Council
  - 28 members
  - meet quarterly
  - Vice President, Personnel a member

[1] An oblique between two titles indicates the two positions are held by one person

> One can place far too much emphasis on the reporting relationship with the chief executive officer. To me (and I report to the CEO), it is important that I have access to the senior decision level of the organization. In practice, our organization has a number of collegial decision forums that are used by the CEO to make his decisions. Access to, and involvement in, these forums is the key.

Said another:

> I report directly to the CEO but I don't expect direct responses from him. He will say: "Let's take it to the policy committee." He will make a decision after the matter has been fully aired by my peers.

Thus while having a direct reporting relationship can be helpful, it is important to look at the reporting relationship in the context of participation in the senior executive council of the organization.

The Senior Decision-Making Council of the Organization

The topic of this section can best be introduced by the following quotation from one of the participants:

> We have two committees at the senior level. One is the policy committee, which does strategic planning and also deals with corporate staff policy matters. This committee consists of the president and chief executive officer, and the four staff executive vice presidents. The other is the executive committee, which meets monthly and includes all of the above as well as the chief executive officers of the major subsidiaries. Membership on these committees has been essential to my doing an effective job of integrating human resources with overall business planning and management.

The senior human resource executive must have access to the senior decision-making council of the organization either through formal membership or other types of involvement.

As might be expected, the senior executive councils of the ten organizations that took part in the study, differed markedly in terms of mandate, size, frequency of meetings and membership. In terms of human resource membership on these councils, Exhibit 7 (middle column) shows the following:

- In four of the organizations, the senior human resource executive was a member of the senior executive council.

- In three of the organizations, the senior human resource executive was not a formal member but either attended almost all meetings or could attend when desired.

- In three of the organizations, the executive was not a formal member but attended when a human resource matter was under consideration.

Either membership or other involvement with the senior executive council on the part of the senior human resource executive does not provide a sufficient basis for effective integration. It is essential that the executive make an important contribution to the council not only in terms of his functional skills but also in terms of his general management skills. In the words of one of the chief executive officers:

> Our senior human resources executive reports to me, and is a member of our policy committee. Given his background and skills, he not only represents the human resource dimension in discussions but also contributes very effectively to other aspects of the business. He is an important member of the policy committee not primarily because of his functional contribution but because he contributes to discussions on general business matters.

Effectiveness on the part of the senior human resource executive (as seen in the above quotation) is a combination of a number of factors including personal effectiveness, professional skills, managerial ability, and a clear understanding of the role of the human resource function. This last aspect will be examined in Chapter VII. Said one of the participants:

> I see my role as one of bringing my skills and experience to bear on policy matters in general. In terms of my functional responsibility at the executive committee level, my role is to ensure that the focus of my function is on meeting the needs of the business.

Other Senior Human Resource Councils

Exhibit 7 (right column) shows other important senior management councils or forums that deal with human resource matters. The exhibit also provides information on the membership on these forums.[6] The one senior executive forum referred to by almost all participants was a human resource planning committee whose primary responsibility was succession planning. Here again, membership, frequency of meetings, and other matters varied considerably. The essence of such committees is captured in this quotation:

> Our senior executive succession planning committee meets four times a year for a day at a time. The committee, which is chaired by the CEO, looks at executive succession planning and development for the top 75 jobs in the company. This brings the matter of succession right into the line organization. Our CEO takes a very direct interest in this area.

Concluding Note

If there is not a direct reporting relationship between the senior human resource executive and the chief executive officer, and the former is not a member of the senior executive decision-making forum, how can effective integration of human resource management with overall business management be provided? Three conditions are considered important:

1. Information flow — There should be effective flow of information between top management and the senior human resource executive. The following comment best describes this point:

---

[6] The forums described in Exhibit 7 are examples and do not represent all possible forums for the ten organizations.

The most important question is one of information flow. It is vitally important that the senior human resource executive be properly "plugged into" the information network in the organization. This includes access to strategic and operational plans and awareness of progress against such plans. It also includes being fully aware of major deliberations in which he does not take part. If you are fully "plugged in," then whom you report to is a lot less important. The important thing is to have access and to have input into deliberations.

A note of caution was added:

There are limits to this. If one reports two or three levels down it becomes much harder to get input. It is not essential that you report directly, but you have to report closely and be linked to all the data and information bases continually.

The senior human resource executive's access to information will be facilitated if he is seen as being helpful to line managers, thus providing a valuable input into the overall effectiveness of the organization.

2. Style of management — Regardless of the reporting structure, the senior human resource executive can develop a working relationship with the chief executive officer and others, which properly provides for effective human resources input. This will occur where the formalities of the hierarchy are downplayed and the management style is informal.

3. The "linking pin" — Where the senior human resource executive is not a member of the senior executive council, the person to whom he reports has an important role to play in linking the senior human resource executive with the senior executive group. One of the participants commented:

The expertise and understanding of the executive that provides the "linking pin" relationship is crucial. Ideally, this individual should have a background in human resources. If this is the case, then there is not the same need for a direct reporting relationship. If the person doesn't have a human resources background, he must have a human resource orientation.

Linkages with Senior Line Managers

These linkages deal with the relationships between the senior human resource executive (and members of his staff) and senior line managers at the corporate as well as at the business unit or subsidiary level. Effective linkages at this level were felt to be of vital importance to meaningful integration. One of the participants commented:

It is important that I have an effective working relationship with those to whom I report. It is equally important, however, that I have effective working relationships with the operating heads of our subsidiaries. These relationships are very critical and if they are working well it makes my job much easier.

Two of the participants in the study described the various ways in which they related to line managers at corporate, as well as at division or subsidiary levels. These examples are meant to provide a perspective on this linkage and are not intended to indicate "best practice." The first example, found in Exhibit 8, outlines the more important councils to which the senior human executive in Organization 4 belongs, as well as other relationships he has developed to assist him in carrying out his mandate. As can be seen, this individual is highly involved with senior operating executives throughout the organization. The second example, taken from Organization 3, outlines various mechanisms the human resource functional executive is involved with, which link the function with the line organization. Exhibit 9 provides a description of these mechanisms, some of which are ongoing while others are project oriented.

These examples demonstrate various ways of ensuring effective integration of human resources with the overall business. These mechanisms are but a starting point. Relationships that flow from these mechanisms are built on the basis of effective contribution to meeting the needs of the particular business from the human resource perspective.

Other Organizational Levels

It is important to have mechanisms in place to ensure effective human resource input into the senior executive decision-making councils. It is equally important to ensure that these same mechanisms are in place at other levels of the organization. Specifically, this refers to human resource input to the decision-making processes within the subsidiary, divisional or business unit levels of the organization and would include plant operations as well as marketing and distribution operations. The same points apply to this discussion as applied at the senior executive level of the organization. In summary:

- It is essential that the functional manager with primary responsibility for human resources is positioned and qualified to be able to contribute to the decision-making processes in his organization.

- It is important that the management committees at the various levels of the organization have proper human resource input into management discussions. One way to ensure that this takes place is through membership on the committee by the human resource professional.

- Membership on such councils, however, is not sufficient to provide proper integration. It is essential that the human resource professional make an effective contribution to the com-

Exhibit 8

Human Resource Linkages with Line Management — Organization 4

Listed below are various internal councils to which the senior human resource executive in this organization belongs. Also described are relationships he has developed to assist in carrying out the function's mandate.

- **Human Resource Planning Group** — This group consists of the Chairman, President, Executive Vice President, Finance and Administration, and Group Vice President, Human Resources. The group meets regularly and reviews all major human resource programs and issues.

- **The Executive Committee** — The senior executive council for the organization, of which the senior human resource executive is not a member but attends most of the meetings.

- **Quarterly Review Meetings** — These were described as follows:

  > In our organization we have quarterly review sessions for all divisions of the company. As the corporate human resource officer, I attend most of these meetings, totalling 36 a year. I take part in discussions of business operations. They keep me well informed on problems and issues, and I use these meetings as a sounding board for ideas I want to test out.

  > One-to-one relationships with the senior operating executives of the divisions are also very important. Although a lot of work is accomplished at the quarterly review sessions it is important that I maintain good individual contacts. This is where I can help them in the use they make of the human resource function.

- **Operations Committee** — This group consists of corporate executives as well as the heads of divisions and subsidiaries of the company. It meets once per month to discuss overall operational issues. The senior human resource executive is a member of this group.

- **Regular Meetings with Senior Line Managers** — These are regular one-to-one meetings with senior line executives for the purpose of maintaining effective integration. Divisions are at various points in their evolution and have different needs. The purpose of these meetings is to ensure that line management is making the most effective use of the function.

- **Human Resource Function and the President** — This relationship is described by the senior human resource executive:

  > The president's first love is human resource management. I, or anyone on my staff, have very easy access to his office. I have a formal meeting with him once per week and usually meet with him at least two other times each week.

Exhibit 9

Human Resource Linkages with Line Management — Organization 3

Listed below are various mechanisms involving the senior human resource functional executive, which link the function to the line organization.

- Development of the strategic plan, which is updated annually.

- Preparation of the annual operating plan with its budgetary and non-budgetary implications.

- Regular meetings of those who report to the chief executive officer.

- Meetings of the company's corporate council, which are held twice a year formally and more often on an informal basis.

- Organizational support for labour negotiations, where both divisional and departmental general managers are highly involved. Responsibilities of line managers and staff in this area are clearly defined.

- Project review teams of vice presidents and general managers of the business to review important human resource issues have been established. Two recent review teams were on equal pay for work of equal value and employee privacy. In the words of the senior human resource executive:

  Through these review teams, senior line managers get deeply involved in the human resource function. These teams act as sounding boards and screens on critical human resource issues, and they serve two purposes. First, the function obtains the wisdom of these people in dealing with the issue; and, second, the function gets support for the output from line managers. When a policy finally comes out, they have a sense of ownership and they get behind it.

- Position guides for the corporate human resource executive and those of the business department general managers, which carefully specify the respective roles in the management of human resources.

- Processes of reviewing all major financial appropriations, which ensure that possible human resource implications have been addressed and plans to manage these aspects exist.

- Staff support for the management development and compensation committee of the board of directors.

mittee. Further, the contribution should extend beyond matters related to the functional speciality to general management issues.

Functional Integration

The last linkage to ensure that human resource considerations are taken into account in all relevant situations is between the senior human resource executive at the corporate level and his staff, and his counterpart executive at the business unit or subsidiary level and his staff. In the majority of cases, the human resource executive of the subsidiary will report to the chief executive officer of the subsidiary and will relate to the corporate human resource executive in a "dotted-line" sense.

Important aspects of functional integration include mutual understanding of the role and responsibilities at various organizational levels within the function. An effective flow of information both from the senior level to other levels and from the business unit levels to the senior levels is also included. This flow is important in terms of input into the planning process at various levels and in the proper resolution of problems. This linkage will be discussed in detail in Chapter IX where the human resource function is examined.

Conclusion

This chapter has demonstrated that in order for effective integration to take place, effective linkages and processes should be in place not only to enhance the contribution of human resource input into the overall business, but also to provide human resource leadership in the planning and management process itself. These linkages have to be in place; they have to be applied in a consistent and continual manner and must be managed effectively.

VI The Chief Executive Officer

Excerpts from a discussion with the chief executive officer of one of the companies involved in the study are as follows:

> The challenges of the 1980s will require a proper orientation towards human resources by the organization. Orientation towards human resources is and will become increasingly critical and this extends to the climate an organization wants to establish. Without proper orientation, techniques are not going to work.
>
> Orientation involves the principles, values, philosophy and beliefs about human resources. It sounds like "motherhood" and sometimes we get embarrassed by motherhood statements but that is where it starts. Senior management must do a lot more thinking about this important area in the future.
>
> The chief executive officer must be clear in his own mind how he thinks about human resources. He has to determine where he sits, and then he has to make certain the organization is aware of this and that he practises it. The chief executive officer must be clear about his personal charter with respect to people.
>
> Another important aspect is the behaviour of the chief executive officer. If he is seen spending his own time on "people" matters then they will be seen as important. The chief executive officer plays an extremely important role in terms of his behaviour.
>
> It is one thing to say that management of human resources is a line reponsibility. It is also important that it be a corporate responsibility. This means placing the responsibility at the most senior levels and managing that responsibility effectively. I am convinced that this will make an organization successful in the long run.

Another chief executive officer whose organization participated in the study said:

> I try to practise an open and caring management style. It is clear to me that I have an important impact on the organization. If we end up with a closed organization, I will have been primarily responsible. Our employees are so important to us. Over and over I emphasize this, both through talking about it and in what I do every day.

These quotations characterize the essence of the fourth principle of the study, which deals with the role of the office of the chief executive officer in integrating overall business planning with the management of human resources.

Principle 4.

> Effective human resource management, in the context of overall business planning and management, will be facilitated to the extent that, *the office of the chief executive officer provides the climate for integrating human resource considerations to the needs of the business.*

The term *provides the climate* refers to the establishment of an atmosphere that supports and reinforces the values and beliefs of the chief executive officer with respect to human resources. Typically, these values and beliefs will be characterized by an atmosphere of openness and trust and of a participative environment where self motivation is valued.

Providing the climate may be the responsibility of more than one senior executive and will depend in part on how the organization is structured around the chief executive officer. This explains why the term *office of the chief executive officer* is used in the principle.

The term *to the needs of the business* means the management of human resources is the responsibility of every manager in the organization and that initiatives in human resource management must relate to the requirements of the business. Initiatives, which are new approaches or revisions to existing practice, can come from a variety of sources. The chief executive officer must ensure that their focus is on the needs and requirements of the business.

The outline for this chapter is as follows: the concept of the office of the chief executive officer is examined first, followed by a discussion of different ways in which the chief executive officer provides the climate. The chapter concludes with an examination of the relationship between the chief executive officer and the senior human resource executive.

Office of the Chief Executive Officer

The use of the term *office of the chief executive officer* refers to an important dimension about managing large organizations. Specifically, the chief executive officer's job is so complex that it is difficult for one person to have total responsibility for providing the climate. The realities of the management of complex organizations suggest that the climate or orientation emerges from a more collegial forum at the top of the organization. In fact, a number of organizations have formalized the concept of the office of the chief executive officer. One such organization was involved in the study.

Exhibit 10 describes the structure of the senior executive group of ten organizations that participated in the research. It shows the title of the senior executive, the nature of his overall responsibilities, and the positions that report directly to him. In Organization 1 the four senior corporate executives operate as a senior executive group, which is in essence a corporate office. The chief executive officer of this organization expressed the following view:

> One can put too much emphasis on the charismatic or leadership qualities of the chief executive officer. In our organization, the four most senior executives, including myself, make up a senior executive group. It is equally important that the other three are as much involved in setting the climate for the organization as it is for me. To the extent that this occurs, the system supports the process as much as it does my leadership.

A similar point about the collegial nature of the senior executive group could be made for other organizations that participated in the study even though the concept of the office of the chief executive officer was not formally used.

Exhibit 10 also shows that in five of the ten organizations (Organizations 1, 2, 5, 9 and 10), the chairman of the board of directors is not a full-time position and the overall operating responsibility for the organization rests with the chief executive officer. In four of the organizations (Organizations 4, 6, 7 and 8), responsibilities are shared between the full-time chairman and the chief executive officer (or president). In each case, it is the latter who has reporting responsibility for human resource management. Therefore, he too will have an important role to play in providing the overall climate. Regardless of titles, or of the concept of shared responsibility at the most senior level of an organization, the fact remains that there is one individual — referred to as the chief executive officer in this chapter — who has a very important role to play in providing the overall climate.

Providing the Climate for the Organization

There are many ways the chief executive officer can provide the proper climate. In this study, two different categories are described: the use of organizational systems and processes, which support the management of human resources, and personal style.

Organizational Processes

All large organizations have a variety of processes to assist in the management of their human resources. The commitment to adhere to these processes will go a long way towards establishing the appropriate climate. This section briefly describes a number of these processes including planning, communication, performance reviewing, the reward system, and succession planning.

Exhibit 10

Structure of the Senior Executive Group of Participating Organizations

Title of Senior Executive(s)[1]	Scope of Responsibilities of the Senior Executive(s)	Reporting Directly to the Senior Executive
Organization 1		
President/Chief Executive Officer	President/Chief Executive Officer has overall responsibility	Three Senior Vice Presidents. The four operate as a corporate office
Organization 2		
President/Chief Executive Officer	President/Chief Executive Officer has overall responsibility	Four Executive Vice Presidents and three corporate Vice Presidents (Corporate Planning, Organization and Management, and Personnel)
Organziation 3		
Chairman of the Board/Chief Executive Officer	Chairman of the Board/Chief Executive Officer has overall responsibility	Three operating Vice Presidents and four corporate staff Vice Presidents (Legal, Strategic Planning and Development, Finance and Human Resources)
Organization 4		
Chairman of the Board/Chief Executive Officer and a President	President has primary operating responsibility	Two Executive Vice Presidents (Finance and Legal), one Operations Group Vice President and a Group Vice President, Human Resources.
Organization 5		
President/Chief Executive Officer	President/Chief Executive Officer has overall responsibility	Executive Vice President, four operating Senior Vice Presidents and two staff Senior Vice Presidents

52

Organization 6		
Chairman of the Board and a President/Chief Executive Officer	President/Chief Executive Officer has overall operating responsibility	One operating Executive Vice President and five staff Vice Presidents (Legal, Public Affairs, Purchasing and Materials, Administration, and Corporate Affairs)
Organization 7		
Chairman of the Board and a President/Chief Executive Officer	President/Chief Executive Officer has overall operating responsibility	Three operating and five corporate staff Executive Vice Presidents (Administration, Marketing, Technology, Operations and Finance) and two Vice Presidents (Corporate Relations, and Legal)
Organization 8		
Chairman of the Board and a President	President has overall operating responsibility	Five Executive Vice Presidents
Organization 9		
President/Chief Executive Officer	President/Chief Executive Officer has overall responsibility	Two operating Vice Presidents and four corporate staff Vice Presidents (Human Resources and Public Affairs, Finance, Business Development, and Legal)
Organization 10		
President/Chief Executive Officer	President/Chief Executive Officer has overall responsibility	One operating Vice President and three corporate staff Vice Presidents (Finance and Administration, Corporate Development, and Personnel)

[1] In this exhibit the position of chairman is shown only if that position is full time. An oblique between two titles indicates the two positions are held by one person.

The Planning Process

Three quotations will demonstrate the role of the chief executive officer in the planning process. The first is from a chief executive officer involved in the study:

> In our organization, the strategic plan and every major plan that is submitted must have a human resource element. I insist on this. We consider human resources in the same way we consider a capital investment or marketing decision.

The second example is from a chief executive officer of another organization:

> In terms of planning, I focus my attention on the critical issues that seriously threaten a business's ability to carry out the strategy required to meet its goals and objectives. I will lend my support for those action plans designed to meet the strategy.
>
> I have a number of processes for ensuring effective human resource input into the strategic plan of the company. These include: (1) measuring the accomplishments of the programs identified to address the issues raised; (2) ensuring that appropriations for funds for projects or programs have a human resource element; and (3) ensuring that position descriptions contain accountability for various aspects of the management of human resources.

The senior human resource executive of the same organization commented:

> Our chief executive officer is very supportive. He is very concerned about the issues that we are addressing and reviews these with myself and other executives on a regular basis. He wants to ensure that human resource matters are given the necessary attention. If I do not provide him with periodic reports on important human resource issues, he is after me.

The final quote from one of the chief executive officers involved in the study relates to approvals for appropriations:

> We have a system whereby all major appropriations must have an employee relations review. We look at each proposal from a union perspective, a salary perspective, wage rates, levels of employment, etc. I will not sign off an appropriation unless it has had this review. There is no doubt in my mind that the process creates a climate right through the organization about the importance of human resources.

Communication

A second process deals with communication. All organizations have well established methods of communicating, which include the use of the organizational hierarchy, written memoranda, staff meetings, organization newsletters, etc. The chief executive officer will use these methods to communicate his concern for human resources. He will also use other methods to aid in developing an understanding about the interests, concerns, and suggestions of employees. These include individual as well as small and large forums where information could be obtained and views expressed.

Exhibit 11 describes a series of approaches employed by one of the chief executive officers whose organization was involved in the study. It describes three different approaches used to facilitate two-way communication between the chief executive officer and members of the organization. The approaches outlined in Exhibit 11 are not unique nor are they meant to indicate "best practice." Each chief executive officer, and each organization, will use similar means to ensure that appropriate communication about interest in and concern for human resources takes place.

Performance Reviewing

One chief executive officer described his approach to performance reviewing as follows:

> To me, performance reviewing is absolutely critical. Apart from the yearly review, I have four individual meetings with each person reporting to me. I place a very high priority on this. At these meetings, we focus on development. I discuss their own training, their career plans, how I see them developing, what they should be considering in terms of internal and external developmental experiences, etc. We also discuss their immediate reports and how these individuals are doing. I really push my people during these reviews.

> I spend a lot of time on the development of my people. To me it is a very important responsibility. Getting involved like I do takes an incredible amount of time but it is worth every second.

Another example is provided by a senior human resource executive:

> Our whole annual staff review process throughout the company (covering 10,000 people) was floundering until our chief executive officer took charge. He took the process seriously and expected all of us to do the same. The personnel function does not take the responsibility for seeing that reviews get done. He and other line managers do. It places the responsibility for managing human resources squarely on the line.

The Reward System

One chief executive officer commented:

> One of the most effective ways of providing the climate is through the reward system. A portion of an individual's salary increase must be related to the management of his human resources. This tends to develop a keen sense of importance in managing these resources.

> I am not as concerned about specific ways of measuring performance in this area as I am about how his organization is developing; is he focusing on the development of his people? What is the general climate in his organization, etc.?

> It is the orientation towards human resources that I am after rather than specific measures of performance in this area.

Exhibit 11

Approaches to Organizational Communication — A Case History — Organization 9

This exhibit describes the approaches used by the chief executive officer to facilitate communications between himself and members of the organization.

The processes in this case history are ones in which the chief executive officer (CEO), by his personal actions, demonstrates an explicit (his) preferred way of managing the business.

These are planned approaches that allow the CEO to remain close to his managerial and professional staff, to gain insight into the needs of the business as seen by members of the organization, and to provide an explicit focus on priorities. In this manner, he establishes the climate he desires.

The approaches include individual meetings, in addition to selective and general "sensing" meetings.

Individual Meetings

This approach is used by the CEO to obtain personalized input from key managers in the organization. These planning and review meetings cover all aspects of the business. Hardly any of these meetings take place without significant time being spent on a discussion of the human resources under the jurisdiction of the manager concerned.

As a result, managers note that the CEO, while paying a lot of attention to volumes, working capital, costs and margins, also pays considerable attention to human resource issues such as performance reviewing, succession planning, safety, employee involvement, management development, etc. Word gets around that the CEO is concerned, and this influences others to pay explicit attention to human resource issues.

Selective "Sensing" Meetings

The following process is utilized to assist the CEO in consulting with a random number of managers about the general direction of the company.

Topics for discussion at "sensing" meetings are selected by the CEO and participants get prior notice. Half-day meetings with approximately 15 managers selected at random provide the forum. During the first part of each meeting, the participants as a group prepare their comments, questions or recommendations for discussion with the CEO. During the second part, the CEO listens, comments on recommendations made and, before leaving the meetings, agrees to the courses of action he plans to follow.

While these "sensing" sessions encompass all aspects of the business, emphasis placed on human resources by participants gets a high priority from the CEO. As a result, the human resource issues become more precisely defined and better focused. This is the climate the CEO wants to create and maintain. These meetings are organized for between five to seven groups yearly.

"Sensing" in Large Groups

The participants in these sessions are all members of the management and professional staff of the Company. The meetings are held once a year.

The following process is used as a means (1) to communicate the key issues for the year ahead, (2) to get a common understanding of the issues, (3) to gain commitment towards the resolution of these issues, (4) to allow the CEO to get a first-hand feeling of management's readiness to pursue these objectives. The following steps describe the process.

The CEO writes to all managers and professionals and communicates the key issues he has defined with his immediate staff.

Meetings for 50 to 70 managers and professional staff are planned for each division or geographic location.

Each person is asked to review the CEO's letter and to discuss its contents with his peers prior to the "sensing" meeting.

Group leaders are selected and trained to lead a workshop of eight to ten people.

The CEO's presentation at each meeting is followed by workshops, which focus on the clarity of the issues and on formulating alternatives or action steps which are then reported to the general meeting. Workshop documentation is prepared for follow-up purposes.

Comment

For the purpose of this research study, the point to be made is that human resource issues receive an equal degree of attention by the CEO as other business issues. The fact that the CEO spends a lot of time deliberately and explicitly discussing human resource issues directly with his management and professional staff sets the tone for follow-up. Support systems, such as succession planning, performance/potential evaluation, and career development plans become important because the CEO talks and acts in a consistent way.

Succession Planning

This last example relates to succession planning in the organization:

> With respect to succession planning, our chief executive officer reviews three indexes with each executive reporting to him. He expects each of us to do the same. First, we are asked to determine pivotal jobs in our areas and how many of these jobs are filled or are about to be filled by superior managers with potential. An index is created of pivotal jobs coming up immediately and over the next two years. Second, we are asked to determine how many managers are in the wrong jobs — such as superior managers in non-pivotal jobs. Third, a number of individuals are selected and in-depth development plans are prepared. The chief executive officer reviews and approves each of these plans.
>
> Every two months, each of us has a one-on-one management review meeting with him and each of these three areas is discussed in detail. By golly, this sets the climate! We are not certain how long it will last but it likely will last as long as he stays involved.

Summary

This section indicates that through various management processes, the proper climate and orientation for effective human resource management can be generally established by the chief executive officer. It is essential that the CEO makes use of and follows the processes that are in place to facilitate effective human resource management. For example, the performance reviewing and development processes should not only be adhered to on whatever basis has been established, but proper follow-up should take place in order to ensure the process becomes an integral part of managing. This will help determine the climate in the longer run.

Personal Style

One of the chief executive officers described style this way:

> The CEO is a symbol and we should never underestimate the symbolic value of the position. To capitalize on this, the CEO needs charisma. Being a technocrat (in human resource matters) is not enough.

The personal style and approach of the chief executive officer contributes to the development of a human resource orientation for the organization. This will be evident in many ways. For example:

> If the president is genuinely committed to creating the appropriate climate, it will be signalled in a lot of little ways. At an executive committee meeting dealing with a capital appropriation, he will enquire about the human resource considerations. When a public affairs issue is being discussed, he will ask how it affects the employees. It is easy to recognize the chief executive officer who has this approach. It will come out in daily actions.

Another perspective was offered:

> In discussing this point, we may be looking for big examples but there may be none. It's really the little things such as "tell me more about this,"

particularly when it is said in the presence of other functional heads. This creates the climate and the interest.

And another:

Climate is something that is nurtured and developed through a series of actions rather than something that is dictatorial or directed in any formal sense. Further, it must be supported not only in the chief executive officer's actions but also by the continuity of his actions.

Finally, with respect to climate, one participant observed:

Climate suggests a proactive stance. This means that the chief executive officer should take initiatives and make suggestions about ways of managing human resources rather than remaining neutral or reacting.

Personal styles and approaches will vary considerably and will cover a wide spectrum of involvement in human resource matters (abdication, passive, neutral, active, aggressive). It is important to recognize that the particular personal approach has an important impact on both the climate and management of human resources in the organization.

A Final Example

Exhibit 12 summarizes a number of points made by another of the chief executive officers involved in the study on his role in providing the climate for integrating human resource consideration to the needs of the business. It includes examples of the use of organizational processes and also illustrates the personal style of the individual.

Concluding Comments

The chief executive officer's job is complex. This chapter has intended to provide the chief executive officer, as well as those aspiring to that position, with information that will enable them to pause and reflect upon their approach to the management of human resources. The following questions may be helpful in this reflection:

- What are my principles, values and beliefs about human resources? Are they well articulated?

- Do those who report to me understand these values and beliefs?

- Does my behaviour support and enhance these values and beliefs? How do I know this?

- What examples are there in the organization that show that my beliefs and values are an important part of the organization's culture?

These questions, it may be noted, are applicable to all managers.

Exhibit 12

Setting the Climate — The Role of the Chief Executive Officer — An Illustration — Organization 2

The following notes summarize the points made by the chief executive officer of one of the participating organizations with respect to his role in setting the climate for effective human resource management.

1. The chief executive officer must:

   - provide the necessary vision for the organization. He has to encourage the organization to develop personnel before the need arises. This involves staying ahead of everyone else in terms of: future personnel needs and future skill needs, and changes in the organizational structure to meet emerging needs.

   - be personnally involved in the selection of key appointments to the organization and not necessarily those appointments that are senior. It is these appointments on which the future of the business rests.

   - have a sound understanding of the personnel system and how it works. We fail at times with some of the techniques we use in areas such as recruiting, selection of college graduates, and moving managers through the system.

   - provide an example for the organization in the area of performance reviewing. It is important that we practise what we preach particularly with respect to performance reviewing. Our salary system, succession planning system and management training system are all tied closely with performance reviewing.

2. In most organizations, we tend to work in a closed system. By this I mean most of the communication, including performance reviewing, is one way. We need to open the process more and provide those who report to us with an opportunity to contribute meaningfully to an assessment of their own performance and to comment, in a constructive manner, on the performance of their managers.

3. Some of the things that I do to provide proper orientation to our human resources include:

- a system of ongoing meetings with the executives of our various unions. I provide them with an overview of our investment plans, employment patterns and other general business matters. This is all done outside the context of the union contract and is designed to keep them informed on management concerns.

- an ongoing system of communications sessions with our foremen. There are 25 in each session and we discuss general problems of the company. I meet with two groups every two months and I find these sessions extremely important in keeping me in touch with their concerns. As well, it demonstrates my interest in their concerns.

- the promotion of the approach we call "organizational transparency." This recognizes that accountability for each manager involves sharing openly all relevant information about the resources that are entrusted to him with his superior, and others with a legitimate interest. This helps to break down barriers when, for example, someone from a corporate staff function wants to discuss performance with a business unit manager. I also practise this at my level in reverse. I want managers to feel they can ask me questions about the management of the resources entrusted to me. If they can feel free about asking the CEO a question, it will make for increased confidence and openness throughout the organization.

- My availability to address general management development courses for our superintendents and supervisors. During each two-week course, I spend the last half day with them listening to presentations and providing them with feedback.

- My involvement with the compensation program for our managerial personnel. We have just revised our incentive program, which puts much more emphasis on the bonus component of total compensation. In the future, a large percentage of the bonus component will be based on how the manager handles human resources in his organization. In addition, I am always pushing our personnel people to ensure that we are on the leading edge of compensation and benefit practices.

Providing the Climate for the Human Resource Function

This final section deals with the relationship between the office of the chief executive officer and the human resource organization, particularly the senior human resource executive. This relationship can have an important impact on the organization's orientation towards human resources. Some aspects of the relationship are professional and task oriented, while others are more personal and informal. The nature of the relationship between the chief executive officer and the human resource organization will be a function of at least three related dimensions:

- the degree to which the chief executive officer (or someone else in the office) focuses on the human resource aspects of the business.

- the chief executive officer's regard for the senior human resource executive in terms of his capabilities as the manager of the function.

- the ability of the two individuals to relate both formally (task orientation) and informally (adviser, counsellor).

The weight or importance of these factors is not likely to be equal, nor is it necessary that they be in order to have an effective relationship. Moreover, the dimensions should not be seen as sequential.

A clear understanding of the role and responsibilities of the human resource executive as well as the function itself is the basis for an effective working relationship. In addition, human resource programs (recruiting, management development, salary administration, etc.) must be operating at high standards. Finally, the function must provide leadership for the organization in terms of change and innovation. With these more formal aspects of the job in place, effective working relationships can be developed and fostered. This will result in confidence and trust, which are important components of maintaining an effective working relationship.

There are instances where the relationship extends beyond the formal to more informal aspects. In such cases, the human resource executive enjoys a rather special relationship with the chief executive officer. This could originate from the chief executive officer's personal interest in the field of human resources. It could also come about because the human resource executive acts as a consultant or adviser with respect to the chief executive officer's own performance. This more informal aspect of the relationship tends to be unique, and where it does occur, the overall relationship between the office of the chief executive officer and the human resource function is enhanced.

In summary, an effective working relationship between the chief executive officer and the senior human resource executive is essential. This relationship is built upon the commitment of the chief executive officer to human resources and a mutual respect for professional management of the function.

VII   Establishing Responsibilities for Human Resource Management

This chapter argues that all management positions in an organization should have a recognized and explicit responsibility for human resources. Furthermore, it is maintained that these responsibilities — and their accountability — should be clearly understood, and that primary responsibility for human resource management rests with operating managers throughout the organization.

The process of defining human resource responsibilities throughout the organization is multi-faceted. This chapter begins with a discussion of the overall organizational process — the method of establishing human resource responsibilities within the context of the organization's business planning framework — and examines this linkage. The process of succession planning as a means for establishing responsibilities is examined next. Finally, the process is examined at the level of the individual manager, where specific responsibilities and accountabilities are established.

Principle 5

> Effective human resource management, in the context of overall business planning and management, is facilitated to the extent that *the organization at all levels establishes responsibilities and accountabilities for human resource management*.

Effective management of human resources is dependent on a clear understanding of responsibilities in this area, and should be seen as an integral part of every manager's job. The organization should establish the proper orientation to support this approach and reinforce it with a variety of techniques to assist managers in carrying out these responsibilities. Initially, there must be an *understanding* of the responsibilities in human resource management, followed by *acceptance* of these responsibilities. These two dimensions are enhanced by developing ways of determining and discussing *accountability* for human resource management on an ongoing basis.

The Business Planning Context

Principle 2 stated, in part, that effective integration of human resources and strategic planning was dependent on a strategic plan that explicitly recognized human resource issues related to strategy. This recognition provides the organizational framework for establishing responsibilities and, indeed, the accountability for human resource management. A similar framework for the operating or current-year planning process is necessary. Thus, the corporate operating plan would include a component on human resources, which would cascade throughout the organization, with a similar component in the subsidiary, business unit and plant level operating plans. One participant commented on this process in his organization:

> Some time ago, senior management recognized the need to identify human resource concerns in the operating plans. We were very light in this area and we could see that it was going to cause us serious problems both operationally and in the long term. We feel now that we are halfway there, and that there is good recognition of human resource concerns in the operating plans.

Another commented:

> The business planning process must specifically require that each unit assess issues in the human resource area (along with all other areas) and develop clearly defined objectives to deal with the issues.

And finally, this conclusion:

> It is very difficult to get good, "gutsy" human resource objectives into the operating plans but when you do, it really pays off.

As these comments indicate, the establishment of human resource objectives for the organization should be integrated with the business planning process. It does not have the same focus if it is seen as a separate process, as is the case in some organizations. The following comment is revealing:

> As a way of getting started with systematic human resource management planning, one of our early steps was to develop a separate manpower planning process throughout the company. The process required that each manager every year address a number of specific areas. These included: a demonstration that the organizational structure of the business was appropriate for the short- and long-range plans; a commentary on the performance, potential, and succession for all managers, and a plan of action for the forthcoming year; and an itemization of any human resource issues or initiatives, that should be addressed.

> These issues were reviewed as they came up through the organization by various levels of management. Finally, the president conducted a series of formal reviews once each year. It would have been preferable to start at this process as an integral part of business planning, but to wait for such logical integration would have taken much longer. We finally reached the point where manpower and business planning were, in fact, directly linked.

Not only should human resource matters be an integral part of business plans, but the process of reviewing performance against objectives must also include a review of the human resource plans.

An Example

Appendix H provides an example from one of the participating organizations, which describes a process of defining human resource objectives in the business plans at the corporate and subsidiary levels. Also included are examples of a number of ongoing performance measures for human resource management.

Succession Planning

Effective succession planning is essential to the long-run viability of all organizations. Most large organizations have a formalized succession planning process and place considerable emphasis on this process to identify its future managers. Succession planning, effectively carried out, places the primary responsibility for the management of human resources where it belongs — with every manager. The organization must provide the proper climate (or orientation) for succession planning as well as tools for implementation. The need for a proper atmosphere is the more important of the two requirements.

There are two significant aspects of succession planning that must be considered. The first is deciding on the appropriate time frame for succession planning and projecting the movement that will have to take place over the time frame to ensure that the right executives are in place at the proper time. This is the quantitative aspect of the process. The second aspect relates to the managerial qualities being sought in the succession process, namely, the selection of managers who have or who can acquire the skills that the organization will require *in the future.* One of the participants stated:

> We all know we have to develop managers to do a better job. However, by and large, we have tended to work on the basis of developing the kind of managers that have been successful in the past. We have made the mistake of assuming that what we need tomorrow is the same as what we needed yesterday. This approach will not be good enough in the future.

The same person went on to describe this problem further:

> It is hard to separate performance from potential because historically we have measured performance on an *assumed* set of qualifications in order to meet the requirements of the job. We have not always clearly stated what these requirements are. Some are easier to measure, and tangible yardsticks have been developed. Others are much harder to measure. We have not really identified or discussed the qualities that the manager has exhibited in achieving his performance.

> Also, we have an added dimension of difficulty with respect to qualities exhibited by the manager. We tend to assess these against an historical as opposed to a shifting set of needs. We have not felt confident, at this time, about bringing out in the assessment process more of the future qualities that will be important for managers to possess.

> Accordingly, someone who performs well at a lower management level may have only 5 to 10 per cent of his performance manifested in the qualities that will be needed in 10 to 15 years.

Responsibilities for Succession Planning — The Starting Point

Where does the responsibility for effective succession planning, particularly in terms of future qualities, lie? In the words of one participant:

> It is an inherent part of the strategic planning process. With strategy, the organization is trying to determine what the organization will be like in the future and an important part of this revolves around the kinds of people that will be needed. It involves looking ahead and identifying the qualities that are going to be required, perhaps to do a different kind of job than is being done now. Thus, overall responsibility is shared among those involved in strategic planning.

Another stated:

> The thrust for this kind of approach comes from our senior executive group that claimed they had done it the hard way and did not want those who were coming behind them to go through the same experience.

Thus, the starting point for establishing responsibilities for succession planning rests with the senior executive group, which provides the framework to enable others to identify their specific responsibilities.

Two Examples

Succession planning is a complex subject and cannot be examined in detail in this study. A perspective on the topic can be provided, however, by examining two somewhat different approaches to succession planning. One describes a project undertaken in one of the participating organizations to identify future managerial requirements; the other describes characteristics that are assessed as part of an ongoing succession planning process.

The first example, taken from Organization 10, is described in Appendix I. In this organization, senior management was concerned about the attributes that would be required of managers who would be heading the enterprise in ten years time. The senior 25 managers undertook a major project, which extended over a two-year period, that was designed to identify a profile of future managers of the organization. This profile would then be used in succession planning. It is interesting to note that the project drew heavily on the work the organization had done in articulating its corporate philosophy as was described in Chapter III.

The second example, taken from Organization 1, presents the guidelines this organization uses in the identification of senior management personnel. This example is described in Appendix J. The examples, shown in Appendices I and J, are not intended to indicate the "best practice" but are intended to provide illustrations of points made in this section.

Summary

Most large organizations have formalized succession planning processes that are used to identify future managers of the business. It is important that these processes be seen as an important focal point for establishing responsibilities and accountability for the management of human resources.

The Individual Manager Context

Responsibilities for human resource management at the individual manager level are addressed in this part of the chapter. A number of organizational processes or techniques used to support the desired orientation are examined, among them: position guidelines or descriptions, specific objectives for managers vis-à-vis their human resource responsibilities, and the performance reviewing and reward processes.

The Manager's Responsibilities

There can be no question that the primary responsibility for the management of human resources rests with all operating managers, whether they be marketing, manufacturing, research, finance, legal or other functions.

The above quotation, from a chief executive officer, underscores the importance of the manager's responsibilities with respect to human resources, stressing that operating managers should not look to the human resource function in the organization to carry out their responsibilities. It is not only important that the point be understood throughout the organization but that it also be actively demonstrated in day-to-day management behaviour. Reinforcement of this point can be greatly enhanced by the climate established by senior management through its behaviour. It is also important that the organization provide guidelines for managers to follow. These guidelines assist in making the human resource component of a manager's job explicit, which in turn assists in defining responsibility and accountability for managers at all levels of the organization.

The process of defining responsibilities and accountabilities is discussed below first in terms of position responsibilities and second in terms of the establishment of objectives.

Defining Responsibilities

It is paramount that managers know what is expected of them and it is important to identify the major components of their job responsibilities including human resources, for which they are held accountable.

The above quotation illustrates the potential role that position guidelines or descriptions can play in identifying and clarifying responsibilities. Position guidelines have been in use for quite some time. Two observations can be made about such descriptions. First, they are much more prevalent at middle and lower levels of management than they are at senior levels, particularly the senior executive group. Second, they tend not to be actively used in the management process. One participant said:

> It takes a disciplined manager to review the position descriptions of his managers with them on a regular basis — say annually. There is no question that it is important to do; however, from my experience, it requires discipline.

On the point of position descriptions at the senior level of the organization, the following quotation is instructive.

> We are just now writing position profiles for the top eight executives in the corporation. Each executive did it individually and they are now being organized in a uniform format. This process is now being undertaken because our new chief executive officer wants to re-examine the total management style of the organization. These profiles had not been prepared before. His plan is to put all of these profiles together in a document that would describe the top management of the corporation. In this way, he hopes this will help establish the management style he wants.

Examples of position descriptions are plentiful. Appendix K shows how one participating organization has attempted to specify responsibilities and accountabilities along with suggested measures of performance. Another example taken verbatim from the position description of the chief executive officer from another participating organization, describes his human resource responsibilities as follows:

> Responsibility for assessing, selecting, developing, motivating and rewarding key staff to assure:
>
> • a high level of managerial productivity
>
> • the best use of individual company resources
>
> • management continuity that fulfils the company's present and future management needs.

Two Guidelines

In describing responsibilities and accountability for human resource management on the part of operating managers, the study found two important points:

1. Every applicable aspect of managing human resources must be made part of a line manager's responsibility. One of the participants expressed this notion as follows:

    > We must squeeze every possible dimension of human resource management into the operating manager's job. Take out only those tasks that must be done by specialists, i.e., compensation design, initial staging of recruiting, etc.

This contradicts the view held in a number of organizations where operating managers have relatively little responsibility as many of the tasks are done by the personnel manager. Another commented:

> The fundamental nature of this point must be underscored. We must return the responsibilities and the skills necessary to do his job in managing human resources to the manager.

2. Managers at the more senior levels, in addition to their ongoing responsibilities in the management of human resources, must also focus on the long-term strategic dimensions of human resource management.

This not only refers to matters such as succession planning, but must also include an awareness of the emerging issues and trends in industrial relations and human resources. In addition, it means taking a leadership position in either the initiation or encouragement of changes. Numerous examples could be cited where operating managers were responsible for initiating changes in various aspects of human resource management — many of them highly innovative.

Clarifying responsibilities in the area of human resource management for all operating managers is only a starting point. Position descriptions can be a useful aid in defining responsibilities. It must be ensured that managers have the necessary skills to carry out these responsibilities and that managerial behaviour of senior executives reinforces the responsibilities that have been identified.

Establishing Objectives

The process and practice of establishing specific objectives for individual operating managers, particularly in the area of human resources, was practised to varying degrees by the ten participating organizations. It was felt that much more needed to be done in this area, particularly at the senior executive level of the organization. Further, the link between human resource objectives and the reward system was felt to be unclear and not well practised. This is an area that is receiving increasing attention in a number of the organizations that participated in this study. All agreed it was a high priority matter. The repercussions of poor practice were described by one of the participants:

> If you do not have specific objectives for individuals to accomplish in the human resource area, they will think their performance is measured on other things and this is where they will concentrate their efforts.

> We found this amply evident in our experience, despite the fact that people were paying lip service (and not cynically) to human resource management. If you examined closely what was happening, if there was nothing in the area of personnel objectives, not much was done.

> Therefore, the impression was created that if senior operating managers did not ask their subordinates to specify human resource objectives, they naturally assumed that management was not interested in them.

There is a very definite linkage in our experience between expectations and behaviour and between behaviour and rewards. It is something that we have to work toward more intensely.

Two Examples

Two examples of setting human resource objectives are provided for illustrative purposes. The first, contained in Appendix L, is taken from an organization where the process of establishing human resource objectives (as part of a management goal-setting process) is highly developed. This appendix shows how the cascading effect of one of the president's human resource goals is translated into a goal for the group vice president and his immediate subordinate.

The second example describes a process in one of the companies to establish corporate objectives and to tie in the personal objectives of the top 250 executives more effectively. This company had an objective-setting system for over ten years and made a number of changes over the years to improve the process. Accomplishment of personal objectives is also used to determine an incentive bonus that is part of the executive incentive program.

Appendix M describes the process as developed to the present time and demonstrates an attempt to ensure that individual objectives are not set in isolation but are made within the context of key corporate objectives. It also shows how personal objectives are reviewed with peers as well as managers.

Rewarding Performance

A manager's responsibility for human resource management must be an integral part of the organization's system of reviewing and rewarding performance. This was stressed by one of the participants who suggested a sub-principle to the main principle of the chapter as follows:

> Effective human resource management... is facilitated to the extent that *the organization has convincing mechanisms to impress upon its managers the importance it attaches to human resource management.*

There are a variety of mechanisms that can be used. Already discussed were the use of position descriptions and objectives. This section briefly examines three other mechanisms.

The first is performance reviewing. All too often, performance reviews tend to focus on quantitatively oriented performance areas, many of which are of a short-term nature. Two comments were offered:

The bulk of a manager's review will be performance oriented in a quantitative sense. Human resource aspects will only focus on extreme instances, i.e., strikes.

Said another:

In too many cases human resource management in performance reviews is "a nod and a wink" and then it's on to current performance!

The participants in the study agreed that a performance review should deal specifically with the management of human resources including managerial style and its impact, the creation of an environment for development and learning, succession planning, and an assessment of the overall climate of the work unit. This discussion has a better chance of having a positive impact if there are some mutually agreed upon expectations at the start of the review period that were discussed periodically during the year. If a manager sees that an important part of his overall performance rating will be based on how effectively he manages the human resources under his charge, he will take seriously his responsibilities in this area.

The second area relates to compensation. As expressed by one of the participants:

Just having it in the position description is not enough. It has to be tied directly to the reward system. The performance of an individual against agreed upon human resource objectives must be explicitly recognized in the reward system.

The chief executive officer of this same organization commented on the impact of a newly introduced executive incentive system:

We introduced a new executive incentive system wherein an individual's bonus in a year will be influenced significantly by how he has managed his human resources, specifically in the area of the development and movement of highly talented personnel. If an executive has had to deal with a number of senior moves in and out of his area, and this has occurred with no disruption, he will be rewarded in his bonus. Other areas included are negotiating skills in collective bargaining, management of the collective agreement, the development of his immediate reports, etc.

It also works on the downside. Where performance has not been good in these same areas, it shows up in the bonus.

Commented another executive:

In reward systems we are far too conservative. We are too cautious, operate on a short-term base and fail to use what may end up to be a very important tool.

The third and last mechanism relates to long-term promotional patterns of executives who manage human resources effectively. Two participants described the process in their organizations. The first commented:

We pay a lot of attention in our reward system to those people who develop others well and who have the facility of developing good people. It does not show up in the pay cheque that year, but it does show up very clearly in the promotional pattern.

When you come to select people for senior positions, you select those who are able to develop a team, even at times if you strip members of that team for other assignments.

In the future, we would like to move more towards immediate financial reward in addition to the more important long-term financial rewards.

The second participant described his organization's approach as follows:

For us, the performance-oriented measures in the job description are not what is important. As well, it is not the importance you attach to performance reviewing. If you want to telegraph something to the entire management population about the importance of human resources, it is through the selection of people to senior jobs.

The other aspects (job descriptions, etc.) help and should be there. These, however, are the formal aspects. The proof is in the promotion of managers who have excelled at managing human resources.

We have a job assignment process for senior jobs in the organization. This is for the top 150 managers. Our president is very highly involved in the process and he reviews anyone who gets assigned to the group.

In connection with our job assignment process, we have developed a general manager profile that tells all managers the skills they should have to aspire to senior positions. Many of these skills relate to the management of human resources.

In our organization, a very clear organizational link is made between the managers who are in the top 130 jobs now, and their known ability in the development of human resources.

Organizations will use some or all of these mechanisms with more emphasis on specific mechanisms, depending on particular circumstances. All participants agreed that the development of *convincing mechanisms* was at an early evolutionary stage and would require much more attention in the future. A final comment is instructive:

The important thing is not the ability to set precise human resource objectives so that they can be measured, but rather to create an environment where managers understand that the management of human resources is important. This is reinforced through the establishment of goals and objectives, where possible, but of equal importance through the behaviour of the senior executives in a variety of ways. It is also reinforced during the performance review process where an executive discusses a manager's human resource responsibilities including succession planning, management development, morale, etc., in considerable depth.

This quotation again refers to the organization's orientation to human resources. The proper orientation, continually reinforced through behaviour, will lead to the desired results. Techniques, such as well-defined responsibilities and objectives, in the absence of the necessary commitment and orientation, will tend to fall into disuse.

Defining Responsibilities — Corporate and Operating Perspectives

One of the participants observed why human resource systems sometimes fail and why managers are reticent to accept responsibilities with respect to human resource management. He commented:

> The reason some human resource systems fail in corporations is because of the tendency to develop human resource policies and tools on a corporate basis for global application and monitoring, as opposed to developing policies and tools for the appropriate levels in the organization. This can result in an abdication of responsibilities for human resource management at the middle and lower levels because it is seen as a corporate system.
>
> We need to develop more effectively responsibility and accountability for human resource management between corporate and operating levels as a start.
>
> Those at the corporate level of the organization are responsible in general for a philosophic umbrella — a setting of the proper climate. This level is also specifically responsible for succession planning for human resources.
>
> At the operating levels, two things should be demanded of managers. They must first contribute to the corporate succession program. (This sets up a potential measure of performance.) Second, they must be held accountable for the perpetuation and the health of their organization.
>
> We have reached a watershed in the management of human resources throughout the line organization. In dealing with human resource responsibilities, we have had a tendency to delegate responsibilities upwards, and our systems and policies tend to reinforce this.
>
> In the future, it will be necessary to more effectively segment responsibilities between the corporate and operating levels.

This organization has been attempting to define authority and responsibility for human resource management between the corporate and senior operating levels. A schematic presentation of this delegation of personnel authority at its present stage of development is shown in Appendix N.

Conclusion

The following quotation perhaps captures the degree to which Principle 5 as discussed in this chapter is managed in many organizations:

> In our organization we are at the crossroads. I can find examples of where we are very poor in this area and also of where we are excellent. Accountability, in many cases, quite frankly comes home to roost at the time of negotiations. The management of a division will come to realize, at the crunch of negotiations, that they have not been doing a good job in management-union relations. In the two or three years between negotiations, we have not stressed the importance of maintaining a good dialogue. This is clearly an area where we have not done a good job in stressing a manager's responsibilities and we must find better ways of doing this.

At the other end of the spectrum, I can think of many examples of excellent acceptance of human resource responsibilities on the part of line managers. Some have to do with quality of working life projects where plant and division managers have taken the initiative to improve the work environment. We are proud of these innovations and need to have more of them.

This chapter has stressed that there must be an initial understanding for human resource responsibilities followed by their acceptance. These two dimensions can be reinforced by developing ways of determining accountability and rewarding performance for effective human resource management.

VIII Human Resource Initiatives

This chapter deals with initiatives in human resource management and argues that these initiatives should be tied to the objectives and needs of the business. This implies that the responsibility for ensuring that initiatives are undertaken is a responsibility of both operating managers and human resource functional managers.

Some implications are made in this chapter with regard to the human resource function. Those involved in the function must understand the needs of the business; this means furthering their ongoing involvement in the management of the business. Moreover, objectives for the human resource function must be tied to objectives of the business and its planning process.

While the responsibility for effective human resource management belongs primarily to line managers, some aspects are shared between line managers and human resource functional managers. This shared responsibility can best be carried out where there is mutual agreement on their respective roles, and where there is competent management in both operations and in the human resource function. The theme is stated in the principle for this chapter as follows:

Principle 6

> Effective human resource management, in the context of overall business planning and management, will be facilitated to the extent that *initiatives in the management of human resources are relevant to the needs of the business.*

This principle is deceptively simple. Its application involves a careful examination of a number of aspects of human resource management in the organization, which are outlined in this chapter. First, an examination of the role of the human resource function as seen by management in all parts of the organization is required. Second, a human resource strategy and objectives for the function that are closely tied with the business strategy and its objectives is necessary. Third, effective structuring and staffing of the human resource function at all levels of the organization is required. Finally, it is important that there be accountability of the function.

Defining the Role

The role of the human resource function is in the process of undergoing a change in many organizations. These changes originated with many senior executives and human resource functional executives who became dissatisfied with the traditional role of the human resource function. The traditional role of reacting to crises, in a time of rapid and unpredictable change, has given way to an emerging role of positive action and leadership. Some examples of the dissatisfaction of executives with their traditional role was provided by a number of the participants. One commented:

> There has been a rampant and an all too generalized problem of personnel professionals becoming enamored with little chunks of technology and seeing these technologies as having a life and meaning of their own. These people render a disservice to the organization because they do not have the overall business focus.

Another said:

> How many times have personnel professionals created their own little empires because they created a dependence on the part of operating managers rather than enhancing the operating managers' self-sufficiency?

A third participant commented:

> There are human resource technicians in all kinds of fields (compensation, labour relations, etc.) who have systematically usurped the responsibilities of operating managers and who carve out their own areas of decision making that are properly and necessarily the domain of the operating manager.

Another of the participants described the change that had taken place in his organization relating to the role of the human resource function:

> In our organization, the human resource function has at times in the past, and on occasion in the present, lapsed into a fire brigade mentality. This has been the result, in part, of the sheer number of crises we have faced. It has also reflected the mentality of some of the practitioners who have likened it to defensive football and to playing the "gatekeeper" role.

> However, in the past few years, through the influence of the strategic planning process and lately through our strategic management focus on resources, the function has been drawn into a proactive stance. As well, the mix of talent and expertise of the employee relations staff has also changed — in the direction of more formal training and more cross-functional experience.

> Employee relations managers now actively participate in the management of our businesses. As well, they compete for resources in the organization through budgets supported by work plans that describe goals, objectives, plans, resources required, and benefits. Accountability is clearly defined and aggressively reviewed against performance.

> Managers in the employee relations function participate not only in support of the business plans, but also in screening business plans — projects and programs to ensure that human resource issues are recognized and resources are put in place to address them.

These quotations underscore the importance of having a clearly defined role for the human resource function. The lack of a well-defined role leads to inappropriate expectations, and in turn to ineffective performance. The definition or redefinition of the role is, however, but a starting point leading to the formulation of strategy, followed by the structuring of the function and to staffing and evaluation.

Case Examples

Examples taken from two of the organizations that took part in the study are highlighted in this section. Each of these organizations recently redefined the role of the corporate human resource function. A discussion of some guidelines that can be used in defining the function's role concludes the section. In Organization 2, redefinition of the role of the corporate personnel function originated from a major corporate project that established the organization's purpose. This in turn led to the definition of the strategic shape of the corporation, which included a section on personnel. This made it possible to redefine the role of the corporate personnel department. (The process of defining the organization's purpose was described in Chapter III, and the strategic shape project was described in Chapter IV.)

Exhibit 13 is an overview statement of the role of the corporate personnel department that was structured to ensure that meeting the needs of the business is the primary responsibility of the function. With respect to the first activity shown in the exhibit, the corporate human resource executive for the organization commented:

> The first activity (meeting corporate requirements) was possible to write out once we had determined the strategic shape of the corporation for the next 20 years. This strategy document had a section on human resources that pointed the way for the personnel function.

The corporate personnel department of this organization has five main functions: personnel and organizational planning and development; research and planning; group compensation and benefits; personnel management communication; and integration and surveillance. Appendix O contains a description of the responsibilities under each of these five functions.

A review of the responsibilities listed under each of the five functions in Appendix O illustrates a number of the points that will be elaborated on in this chapter:

- Corporate personnel strategy is closely tied to business strategy (Function 1, III).

- Personnel function managers are to play an active part in the management of the business units they service (1, IV).

- The function must be proactive and take a long-term perspective (2, various aspects).

The second example is taken from Organization 4. In this organization, the senior executive management committee requested a review of the role of the corporate human resource function. The executive committee felt that, in the future, the role of the human resource function must be conceived in a way that:

(a) accounts for the efficient functioning of human resource management in the company.

(b) ensures the optimal utilization of internal and external information concerning trends in the labour force and among the company's human resources.

(c) provides a broad-based link between the company and other successful large organizations with regard to human resources.

(d) opens avenues of exchange with the environment. This will involve participation in networks in the political system, as well as the professional and educational fields.

The senior corporate human resource executive who fully supported and encouraged the review commented:

What was new and exciting about this perspective, which was taken with regard to the role, was the increased sensitivity of the company towards the need to relate directly to the environment.

We have always been a progressive and innovative organization in terms of human resources, which has been reflected in many organizational and management projects, including quality of working life, a computerized personnel management information system, a senior job assignment process, a senior management assessment process, etc.

However, we are aware that these innovations will not suffice. Things are changing too fast, and the framework within which our human resource policies and practices will evolve is ambiguous and uncertain. Federal and provincial legislation in areas such as language, equal opportunity, health and safety, to take just three, is having a major impact on us. As well, changes in the labour force are affecting us and will continue to do so.

These were but a few of the elements that led to the redefinition of my role and the role of corporate human resources.

The review of the human resource function's role involved a variety of groups and individuals in the organization including the executive committee, the staff of the corporate personnel group, the senior staff of the various operating divisions, and the personnel division heads. The following questions were asked during the review:

- What work needs to be done?
- For whom?
- In what configuration of relationships?
- With what authority and responsibility?
- Under what priorities?

Appendix P describes the redefined role of the corporate human resource function. The role statement defines six major areas. The senior human resource executive commented on what occurred after completion of the role definition exercise:

Following the redefinition of the role, the executive committee assigned a number of priorities for the function. These priorities were put into a three-year plan and focused on five main areas: (1) staffing of senior jobs through the job assignment process; (2) developing certain minimum company-wide human resource policies; (3) making external advice available to various levels of management (which we strongly encourage); (4) helping operating managers make optimal use of the human resource function. This priority is very important and has taken as much time as all the others together; (5) linking up with selected aspects of the external environment (belonging to and taking an active part in a number of groups).

Some Guidelines

The study participants believed a number of guidelines suggested by the study could be of assistance in (1) defining or redefining the role of the human resource function, and in (2) determining responsibilities for human resource initiatives between operating or line managers, and human resource functional managers.

1.   Guidelines Relating to Defining the Role of the Function

●   *Meeting Business Needs* — The direction and activities of the human resource function should be geared toward meeting the objectives and needs of the business. This was described by one participant as the concept of *organizational readiness* — the ability of the function to be responsive to the needs of the business.

In order to meet this guideline, a number of things are necessary. First, the human resource function must be closely tied both to the strategic and operational business planning process as discussed in Chapter IV. Second, the human resource function must be effectively linked with the organization at various levels as discussed in Chapter V. Third, the function must be staffed with high calibre managers. (This topic is addressed later in this chapter.)

●   *Three Dimensions of the Role* — The first dimension of the role is to provide professional functional expertise throughout the organization. This is done by ensuring that human resource systems (recruiting, development, compensation, etc.) are operating in an efficient and effective manner. The second dimension of the role of the human resource function is to provide leadership in its areas of expertise by pointing out new initiatives that can be undertaken, and by ensuring that the organization anticipates changes rather than reacting to them. The third dimension of the role is for the function to play an effective part in the management team at every level of the organization.

●   *The Organization's Environments* — This guideline relates to the organization's environments and suggests that the human resource function must monitor the internal and external environments on an ongoing basis. Trends in these environments must be analyzed with regard to their impact and dealt with at appropriate levels of the organization.

2.   Guidelines Relating to Responsibilities for Initiatives

●   *A Shared Responsibility* — While the primary responsibility for human resource management rests with operating managers, some aspects are shared. Ensuring that initiatives reflect the needs of the business is an example of a shared responsibility. This can best be done where there is mutual agreement on respective roles and where there is competent management in both the operating part of the organization and in the function.

●   *Two Needs To Be Satisfied* — Both operating managers and human resource specialists need to execute the basics in human resource management satisfactorily. This means that day-to-day maintenance type activities of the function are performed according to high standards. This includes the smooth operation of human resource systems in areas such as recruiting and selection, development, compensation, performance reviewing, administration of collective agreements, etc. The second need is to ensure that periodic initiatives be undertaken to assist the organization in the continual process of adapting to its changing environment. Operating managers have a right to expect that the systems be in place to meet the first need. They also have a responsibility to ensure that initiatives take place. Leadership by operating managers will pay high dividends in this area. The task is not to be conversant with solutions, but rather to be cognizant of a potential problem or a missed opportunity.

Planning in the Human Resource Function

Once the role of the human resource function has been defined, it is possible to determine the strategy. The study found that it was essential to have a well conceived planning process in human resources including a strategic plan. This section, therefore, discusses the planning process for the human resource function at the corporate and business unit levels. Human resource planning is closely tied to strategic and operational planning for the organization as a whole, as discussed in Chapter IV. Examples taken from three of the participating organizations are used to illustrate the planning process in the human resource function and includes parts of the actual plans.

Example 1 — Organization 7

This example illustrates the human resource planning cycle and is taken from Organization 7.[1] The objective of the human resource planning process for this organization is to ensure that:

- continuous and systematic attention is given to human resource strategic and business planning,

- effective interfaces are developed and maintained between the corporate office and the subsidiaries in planning,

- sufficient resources are directed towards resolving priority issues/opportunities affecting the business.

The human resource planning cycle is depicted in Exhibit 14. This cycle provides for both corporate and subsidiary exchange of information on international, national and local key issues/concerns

---

[1] The corporate strategic planning process for this organization was described in Chapter IV (Example 4, Organization 7). This description showed how human resource planning was integrated with overall strategic planning for the corporation. It also showed the key human resource elements of the corporate strategic plan. The description in the present chapter focuses on the human resource planning process between the corporate and subsidiary levels.

Exhibit 14
Human Resource Planning Cycle, Corporate and Subsidiary Levels — Organization 7

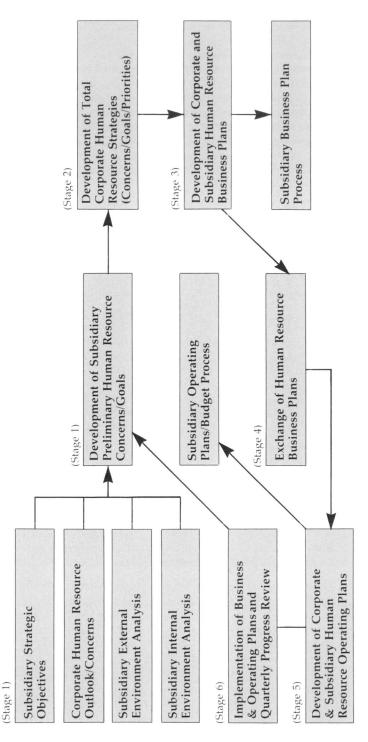

(Stage 1)

Subsidiary Strategic Objectives

Corporate Human Resource Outlook/Concerns

Subsidiary External Environment Analysis

Subsidiary Internal Environment Analysis

(Stage 1)

Development of Subsidiary Preliminary Human Resource Concerns/Goals

(Stage 2)

Development of Total Corporate Human Resource Strategies (Concerns/Goals/Priorities)

(Stage 3)

Development of Corporate and Subsidiary Human Resource Business Plans

Subsidiary Business Plan Process

Subsidiary Operating Plans/Budget Process

(Stage 4)

Exchange of Human Resource Business Plans

(Stage 6)

Implementation of Business & Operating Plans and Quarterly Progress Review

(Stage 5)

Development of Corporate & Subsidiary Human Resource Operating Plans

Source: Organization 7; The Conference Board of Canada

84

and their probable impact on the corporation (stage 1). Preliminary human resource concerns/goals for each subsidiary are then developed (stage 1). Those issues/concerns having broad corporate impact are given priority and corporate-wide human resource strategies are developed (stage 2). The output of stage 2 is used by the corporation and each subsidiary as the basis for developing their five-year business plans (stage 3). Next, the human resource business plans for all units are exchanged (stage 4). The last two stages of the process relate to the development and implementation of corporate and subsidiary human resource operating plans (stages 5 and 6). The process is described in more detail in Appendix Q. The senior human resource executive summarized the impact of the process as follows:

> Within the company, there is no question that human resource management is seen as a key and critical element in the success or failure of meeting business objectives. Over the last few years, this has changed from being a simple truism, to being a major concern, and to being a strategic issue of equal importance with marketing and technology. We have a long way to go in identifying the long-term critical issues and concerns and successfully implementing appropriate strategies.

Example 2 — Organization 10

In Organization 10, the planning process for the corporate human resource function includes the identification of corporate human resource strategic issues that will require attention during the year. These issues are based on an assessment of corporate needs, which includes an analysis of issues and trends in the internal and external environments of the organization. The strategic issues for 1980 are shown in Appendix R and include four areas: corporate functional capabilities, manpower, compensation and benefits, and employee relations. Also shown in Appendix R are examples of 1980 corporate human resource goals. These goals are derived from the strategic issues and are accompanied by specific measures that can be used to determine whether or not the goal has been accomplished, as well as milestones to be achieved in their accomplishment. Finally, Appendix R shows the 1981 corporate strategic human resource issues, which is part of the overall corporate strategic plan for 1981, and the starting point for developing the 1981 corporate human resource goals.

Example 3 — Organization 2

The third and final example presents the corporate personnel strategy for another organization that participated in the study. This strategy flowed from the role of the function (described earlier in this chapter), as well as corporate strategy (described in Chapter IV) and corporate purpose (outlined in Chapter III). The corporate personnel strategy as described in Appendix S includes five areas:

- implementation of a process for better development of international management resources of the corporation,

- assessment of the need for management renewal through external recruiting at senior levels,

- re-establishment of the corporation's reputation as an innovator in "people management,"

- implementation of the "people dimensions" of the corporate purpose statement and assessment of the effectiveness in attaining these dimensions,

- improvement of the organization's health and safety program.

Some Observations

The examples in this section examined human resource planning from two perspectives. First, the *process* of human resource planning; and second, the *content* of corporate human resource plans. The participants in the study felt that a number of observations could be made about human resource planning, as follows:

- Effective strategic planning in the human resource function is dependent on effective strategic planning for the organization as a whole. The examples in this chapter underscore the importance of the relationship between human resource planning and overall strategic planning.

- Strategic planning in the human resource function is closely related to the function's mission, which must be related to the needs of the business.

- The relationship between human resource planning and management at the corporate and subsidiary or division levels is important. There must be effective processes to link the more broadly based corporate issues and goals with subsidiary plans. This point is elaborated on in the following section.

Managing the Human Resource Function — Some Important Dimensions

The principle of this chapter, and the discussion up to this point, raises a number of questions about the management of the human resource function. Three questions examined in the course of the research and discussed next are: (1) How should the function be structured to achieve its mission? (2) What kinds of skills are needed in the function? (3) How should the function evaluate its effectiveness?

Structuring the Function

The effective operation of the human resource function in large organizations depends in part on the appropriate division of responsibilities among various levels of the organization. On what basis, for example, should responsibilities be divided between the corporate human resource activity and that of other parts of the organization (groups, divisions, business units, plants, etc.)? A number of the organizations that participated in the study had, in the recent past, addressed this question. One of the participants described his thoughts this way:

> We had a problem of balance between corporate and divisional levels. Historically, in our organization, a lot of corporate activity was operational. Accordingly, the divisional people had to do a lot of *ad hoc* policy making.

> We discovered that because the corporate level was too involved with day-to-day operating issues, it was not doing the necessary policy work. This created a policy vacuum at the divisional levels, which led them to make these *ad hoc* decisions.

> We decided that we had to provide leadership by doing what was appropriate at the corporate level. Recently, we have been going through a process of identifying corporate policy directions.

> At this time, we have agreed that the role of the corporate unit is to. plan ahead, conduct research, carry out a certain amount of monitoring, develop policy positions for corporate approval, and provide certain kinds of direct assistance to divisions, as needed.

The following examples describe how two organizations delineate responsibilities at the corporate and divisional levels. The first example is taken from Organization 8. The general division of authority between the corporate and divisional human resource functions is shown in Appendix T. This example represents an attempt to focus the corporate role on overall organization-wide concerns. The senior human resource executive commented:

> This division of authority required a lot of thinking and discussion within the function at the corporate and divisional levels. The division works quite well in practice. Confusion at times occurs; however, it is resolved by open discussion which requires effective "boundary management" by both groups.

The second example — an organization chart — is presented in Appendix U. This company is a large manufacturing organization. The first part of Appendix U portrays the corporate employee relations function. It shows a distinction between what is referred to as *operating work* and *staff work*. The majority of the time, it was reported, was spent on the latter. The corporate employee relations vice president commented:

> The corporate role basically assures that corporate standards are met, ensures that consistency prevails on major items, and provides advice and counsel when requested or when required.

In general, corporate issues are strategic issues. These are major changes in direction or new programs.

Strategy in this sense refers to an issue that, if not addressed, will seriously impede the ability of the business to meet its objectives. Examples are:

(1) Manpower: Do we have enough managers available to meet the corporation's export thrusts?

(2) Productivity: To meet international competition in the new GATT environment, how will technology and human resource interfaces be managed to maximum advantage?

(3) Job security: How can employee support be maintained for evolving changes in corporate structure (exits, mergers, etc.)?

Finally, we must be sure that strategic issues come up from the business units as well as those issues we identify at the corporate level.

The division of responsibilities between the corporate human resource function and the business unit counterparts depend on many factors. Discussion during the study, however, provided the basis for the following observations:

- The corporate role should focus on policies, planning and co-ordination. These activities require constant focus on strategic issues facing the organization that will have an enduring effect upon its future. Said one participant:

  In our organization, we attempt to divide responsibilities on a time-frame basis. The corporate level should be dealing with long-term strategic matters. They will also have short-term time frame matters but most of the thinking will be long term. By the same token, while plant operations should be focusing on a shorter term time horizon, some attention must be given to the longer term.

- There is an increasing amount of attention at the corporate level on environmental analysis and research. This appears to have come about from the realization that research into human resource matters is as important as product or consumer research. This increased attention remains a "tip of the iceberg effort," however.

- The identification of strategic concerns is not restricted to the corporate level. All levels of the function should contribute to an assessment of forthcoming issues that may have significant impact on the organization.

Staffing the Human Resource Function

Managers in the human resource function must be business managers first and specialists second.

This quotation captures the sentiments of the human resource executives that participated in the study. One of the participants described this as follows:

The managerial skills required by the operating manager and the human resource manager are no different. First a manager, then a role.

What do these quotations suggest about the skills of human resource managers? They suggest that the human resource manager views himself as a manager of the business first and as a specialist second. This means two things. First, the human resource manager must contribute to the overall management of the business at his level. He must take an active part in the management of the business and not contribute solely to matters related to his speciality. Second, he must manage his function to the same skill level required of business unit managers. Thus, for example, the function would undertake a strategic analysis of its "product" (the service provided) and its "customers" (the business units being served). In summary, a human resource manager who is a skilled personnel professional but lacks in overall managerial expertise, will not be able to contribute to management of the business.

How can these skills be obtained? A number of organizations have responded to this question by ensuring that the human resource function is staffed with a blend of individuals who have had good managerial experience in other parts of the organization as well as those who are career professionals in human resources. Four organizations that participated in the study have a policy whereby the senior human resource executive at the corporate level is an individual with excellent line experience, who is likely to be a candidate for senior management succession in the future. This position tends to rotate every three or four years. In these organizations, where appropriate, career personnel professionals are provided with an opportunity to obtain operating experience at one or more points in their careers. Organizations in the study not having this policy believe it is important that the human resource function be staffed with a blend of individuals with both operating and functional human resource experience.

This blend of individuals with operating management experience and functional expertise assists in directing the activities of the function towards:

- initiatives that meet the needs of the business,

- programs that not only respond to crises but anticipate problem areas or break new ground,

- initiatives that are undertaken only if the basic functional services are being performed at high standards,

- creation of self-sufficiency in the line organization rather than dependency.

One of the participants related the philosophy of his organization in staffing the personnel function, particularly at the corporate level:

As a result of many years of experience, we have developed a series of guidelines to follow in identifying candidates for staffing the personnel department at corporate and divisional levels. These guidelines are as follows:

(1) With a few exceptions, the department should be staffed with managers who have a prior record of operational competence. There is a lot of stock in having people know what happens in the trenches. Exceptions to this are career professionals who are needed in areas such as salary and benefit design.

(2) Human resource functional managers should be rotated every four to six years to keep them operationally up-to-date.

(3) Managers in the department must be well respected by the organization they serve.

(4) Managers must be malleable and broad thinking because the boundaries between the corporate and divisional levels in the function as well as between the function and operations are fuzzy.

(5) Managers must be aggressive but smooth salesmen since they lack the "raw authority" to make things happen.

These guidelines are well established in our organization and have been followed.

One final quote summarizes this discussion on skills required by human resource managers:

I see two rather different skills that the human resource manager must possess. First, he must have the ability to perceive and manage the various specialized components of the function's programs, with the aim of supporting and reinforcing the concept of manpower as a resource, not as something to be administered or controlled. Second, he must possess the ability of an educator to assist operating managers in identifying and solving problems using practical solutions.

Assessing Effectiveness

Effective human resource management in the function must be performed with as much accountability as in any other area.

The primary responsibility for the management of human resources in many organizations lies with operating managers who are accountable for this aspect of the overall performance of their business. How then is the contribution of the human resource function assessed? Two approaches were discussed in the course of the study. Taken together, these approaches to assessing effectiveness can prove useful:

● Assessment of programs and budgets — Where quantitative-oriented objectives have been established, the achievement of these program or project objectives can be one measure of assessment. Monthly activity reports, in use in a number of organizations, are designed to report on the progress of specified projects. Conditions under which the project was or was not accomplished are an important consideration.

- Joint assessments and audits — There is usually a sharing in the development and operation of human resource programs with operating management. Accordingly, there can be a sharing in the accountability for the results. Periodic joint assessments or audits of programs in effect, and diagnostic evaluations will lead to mutually acceptable adaptations and changes.

Two dangers inherent in assessing the contribution of the human resource function were discussed. Measuring effectiveness in negative terms — things or events that did not occur — is one of them, and linking any specific human resource activity with company performance is another. Cause and effect relationships are far more complex than simple relationships may purport.

In the final analysis, accountability depends upon mutual understanding of the respective roles of operating and functional executives in the management of human resources. The assessment process can be facilitated if there is a commitment to encourage constructive criticism of human resource programs. In this way, the human resource executive can operate on the basis of making a contribution in a supportive environment, which is conducive to adaptation and change.

Conclusion

Initiatives in the management of the organization's human resources are of critical importance. Responsibilities for ensuring that initiatives take place should be shared. This shared responsibility can best be carried out where there is mutual agreement on respective roles, particularly at the corporate level, and where competent management in both operations and in the human resource function exists throughout the organization.

IX Dealing with the Organization's Environments

Organizations do not operate in a vacuum. They operate in a complex and ever changing environmental setting. An organization's environments, both external and internal, have an important impact on its operations and, in the final analysis, on its ability to survive. Therefore, it is not surprising that there has recently been heightened interest on the part of many organizations in discovering better ways of understanding and dealing with the various segments of its environments.

The importance of the organization's environments has been discussed throughout this study. Chapter I examined how the environment was addressed in statements of corporate purpose. Chapter II discussed how strategic planning involved a careful assessment of issues and trends in the environment. Chapter VIII dealt with environmental analysis in defining the role of the human resource function.

This chapter deals specifically with the organization's environments, the last of the seven principles of the study. This principle, however, should not be viewed as being the last step in the process of integrating human resources with strategic planning, but rather as the step that completes a cycle that began with defining organizational purpose. Environmental analysis has an important impact on this and other principles of the study.

Principle 7

> Effective human resource management, in the context of overall business planning and management, is facilitated to the extent that *it includes the responsibility to identify and interact in the social, political, technological and economic environments in which the organization is and will be doing business.*

The chapter examines a number of dimensions of environmental analysis in the context of the study. First, responsibility for identifying and managing environmental issues that are likely to have an impact on the organization is examined. Second, different approaches to organizing and integrating the results of environmental monitoring into the organization are assessed. Finally, monitoring human resource environments is examined.

Environmental Monitoring — Whose Responsibility?

Environmental monitoring is the responsibility of all managers in the organization. For many senior executives, a key responsibility includes making effective use of a variety of sources outside the organization to observe trends and issues in the social, political, technological, and economic environments and analyzing their potential impact on the organization in the short and long term. Equally important is the responsibility to monitor the organization's internal environment. For managers at other levels of the organization, the emphasis placed on environmental monitoring will vary by level and function. For more junior managers, such monitoring is likely to be directed towards the internal environment.

The participants in the study concluded that the primary responsibility for creating the proper *orientation* towards environmental monitoring belonged to the senior executive group of the organization. This group sets the stage by stressing the importance of a proper ongoing assessment of the social, political, technological and economic environments in which the organization operates. The chief executive officer plays an important role in this regard. Finally, the orientation must not only be viewed as solely defensive. In many instances, an assessment of the environment will identify opportunities to take advantage of pending changes.

Organizing For Environmental Monitoring

How do companies organize themselves to effectively monitor their environments?[1] A variety of approaches are available, including the role played by the senior executive group, the use of a central monitoring function such as corporate planning or public affairs, the use of the planning process, and assigning responsibility to major functional groups within the organization (finance and human resources, for example). These approaches are not mutually exclusive; an organization may make use of some or all of them. The approaches used will be determined by factors such as the profile and public visibility of the organization and industry, i.e., energy or consumer-oriented companies, the size of the organization, and the style of management of the organization. The approaches described in this chapter are intended to provide examples and are not intended to indicate the "best practice."

---

[1] The discussion in this section can be supplemented by three recent studies by the Conference Board: Rochelle O'Connor, *Planning Under Uncertainty: Multiple Scenarios and Contingency Planning* (New York: The Conference Board, Inc., 1978); James K. Brown, *The Business of Issues: Coping with the Company's Environments* (New York: The Conference Board, Inc., 1980); James K. Brown, *Guidelines for Managing Corporate Issue Programs* (New York: The Conference Board, Inc., 1981).

The Senior Executive Group

The senior executive group has a very important role to play in systematically focusing on the organization's environments, both in terms of assessing trends and analyzing the impact of these trends on the organization. One participant remarked:

> In our organization, one of the most effective ways of keeping abreast of environmental issues is to be part of the senior management group of the organization. Our chief executive officer has a most effective way of ensuring that we discuss trends in a wide variety of areas. Each member of the senior group has his own information network and each of us is encouraged to contribute to the process. Issues that are identified as important are examined in some depth by a team or a particular department. The system works very well.

The chief executive officer and other senior executives have an important role to play not only in identifying and assessing trends but also in interacting with the organization's environments. This interaction depends on the issue, and can range from a more passive to a more aggressive interaction designed to influence a particular environment.

This approach may, in some instances, be the primary monitoring process used by an organization and can work effectively if responsibilities are clearly understood and individuals are skilled at issue identification and analysis.

Central Monitoring Activity

A second approach is to assign primary responsibility for gathering and analyzing environmental information to a central monitoring function or perhaps more than one function. This relates primarily to external environmental information. The public affairs or corporate planning units could be assigned these responsibilities. In such cases, their responsibilities would be to monitor the social, economic, political, and technological environments of the organization using a variety of techniques, and to undertake preliminary issue identification and analysis. Significant issues are assessed in terms of their likely impact and the course of action decided upon by the senior management group. Organizations that use central monitoring agencies are likely to be those that are in high profile industries.

Two organizations that took part in the study recently reorganized a portion of the corporate office resources to more effectively co-ordinate their efforts at managing the relationship between the organization and its environments. In one organization, the corporate human resource function and the public affairs function were reorganized under one senior executive — a vice president, corporate and employee relations. Because of a number of generic similarities between the two functions (responsibility for various aspects of communication, environmental sensing, etc.), a more effective focus on the task of environmental analysis could be developed with the new structure.

In the case of the second organization, three corporate activities namely, human resources, public affairs and corporate strategies were brought together under a new position — a vice president of corporate development. A fundamental reason for the reorganization was to focus more sharply on the organization's efforts at environmental analysis. It is likely that more such reorganizations will take place in the future.

The Planning Process

Central to the strategic planning process is an environmental analysis. One of the participants commented:

> In our organization, environmental sensing is fundamental to the strategic planning process and involves both line managers and functional managers.

The role of environmental analysis in strategic planning has been illustrated throughout this report. The case examples provided in Chapter IV (in particular, Exhibits 3 and 4) describe the role of environmental analysis in both the business planning and human resource planning processes. In Chapter VIII (Exhibit 14), external and internal environmental analysis in the context of a human resource planning cycle was described. These examples demonstrated the importance of environmental analysis in strategic planning. Environmental analysis prepared for the strategic planning process must be reviewed periodically to determine whether issues or their importance have changed.

Functional Responsibility

A further approach ensures that each function of the organization makes the monitoring of its relevant environments one of its key roles. This is particularly true of corporate functions such as finance, human resources and public affairs, but is especially important for business units.

An example provided in the last chapter demonstrates the importance of analyzing trends and emerging issues in the organization's environments. The first statement of the description of the role of the corporate personnel department, shown in full in Appendix P, is presented below:

1. To forecast, conceptualize, plan for and initiate programs on priority problems and emerging issues in the area of human resources.

    • Gather information

    • Acquaint top management with needed changes and reorientation

- Develop relevant action programs in areas such as: legislation affecting the field, labour market characteristics, social trends in other countries, morale and attitudes (of employees), management continuity, optimal utilization of human resources, and conceptual and technical innovations in the field.

This statement illustrates the importance of environmental monitoring for the corporate human resource department of this organization.

Putting It All Together

The various approaches to organizing for environmental analysis should not be viewed as mutually exclusive methods. As mentioned, a particular organization could make use of all of the approaches described. This multi-faceted approach was described by one of the participants as follows:

> Exposure to the internal and external environments is spread widely throughout our corporation. It is, however, the responsibility of the staff function to develop the systems through which widespread sensing is brought into useful focus. The accompanying diagram (Exhibit 15) summarizes the process as it works in our organization.
>
> The identification of emerging societal trends (see (1) in Exhibit 15) and of social planning premises and key issues (2) is the result of interactions stimulated by the staff functions and co-ordinated by corporate planning, which plays an important staff-to-staff role in the process. They organize and lead meetings, provide evaluations of outside assessment services, etc.
>
> The social planning premises and key issues are then discussed with the senior operations vice presidents. Any refinements are made and then discussed with the senior executive policy committee once a year as part of the planning process. (Examples of social planning premises and key issues as they relate to human resources are shown in Exhibit 16.)
>
> The premises and issues, once agreed upon, are analyzed to develop strategies to deal with the issues (see (3) in Exhbit 15). These strategies developed by the staff departments and corporate planning are then cycled through the functional vice presidents and the senior executive group. This step is necessary because implicit in the strategy is the expenditure of time and money.
>
> The structures then become part of the corporation's overall strategic planning document, referred to as the executive planning statement (4). The final step in the process is the implementation of the strategy through policies and programs (5).

This example provides an illustration of how environmental issues are managed in a pragmatic way. Effective management of environmental issues is as important as their identification.

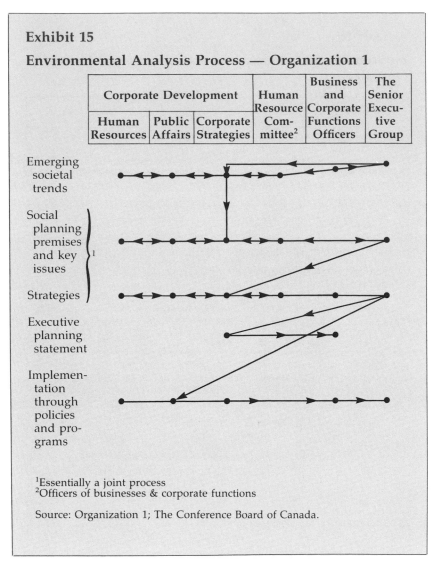

Exhibit 15

Environmental Analysis Process — Organization 1

Corporate Development			Human Resource Com-mittee[2]	Business and Corporate Functions Officers	The Senior Execu-tive Group
Human Resources	Public Affairs	Corporate Strategies			

Emerging societal trends

Social planning premises and key issues

Strategies

$\left.\begin{array}{l} \\ \\ \\ \\ \\ \end{array}\right\}$[1]

Executive planning statement

Implementation through policies and programs

[1]Essentially a joint process
[2]Officers of businesses & corporate functions

Source: Organization 1; The Conference Board of Canada.

Conclusions

What conclusions emerge from the foregoing description of different approaches to organizing for effective environmental analysis? Five points were agreed upon by the participants:

- Effective environmental analysis is dependent on the necessary orientation to this activity. This orientation is established by the senior executive group.

- Monitoring the organization's environments must be seen as part of a manager's responsibilities. This will be rendered

Exhibit 16

Environmental Premises and Issues — Partial Listing — Organization 1

PREMISES	ISSUES
Industrial Relations • Continuing wage competition and work stoppages due to labour and management fragmentation and post-AIB structural vacuum.	• Encouragement of union consolidation and broader based bargaining.
Wages & Salaries • Continued pressure for further income redistribution. • Changing pattern of regional differences.	• To maintain adequate motivation for outstanding contributors and to justify this to the public, as necessary. • Pressure for disclosure of individual management incomes. • To remain reasonably competitive in high wage areas while avoiding national spread.
Employee Benefits • Trend toward higher benefit costs will continue.	• Acceptance of total compensation, rather than basic wage cost as the basis for labour negotiations. • Inclusion of benefits in labour agreements. • Labour pressure for participation in the management of pension funds.
Differential in Rates of Growth • Differential in rates of growth in various business sectors will require different management approaches.	• Organization and supportive policies best suited to managing divergent businesses versus corporate integrity.

easier by the creation of the proper orientation in the organization.

- The time horizon for environmental monitoring must be carefully considered. One of the participants commented:

  > It is important to hold the time frame of future scanning to a time frame that managers can relate to. If it gets out too far, they have a hard time seeing the impact on the organization.

  > In our organization, each major business unit prepared a document (with the assistance of corporate staff) of the key social/political/technological/economic factors that may influence it over the strategic planning horizon, which is five to ten years.

- Analysis of the organization's environments requires a disciplined and systematic approach. It is no longer possible to rely on one or two individuals to assume this responsibility. The approach chosen by an organization should be one that meets its special requirements.

- The human resource function has a responsibility to identify emerging issues and trends in its environments as part of the overall environmental analysis process. The human resource monitoring process should include an identification of the issues, an analysis of their likely impact on the organization, and consideration of strategic responses.

Monitoring the Human Resource Environments

With respect to monitoring the human resource environments one of the participants said:

> From our experience, the area of the organization that is hit most often by social and political developments, and with the most intensity, is the human resource area.

Given the rapid changes that are taking place in areas that have an impact on human resources, both externally and internally, it is important that the human resource function has a clearly identified process in place to monitor its environments. This process would include techniques to monitor the internal and external environments and to integrate the resulting analysis into the decision-making processes of the organization. Those who participated in the study argued that such processes in the human resource function in their organizations were not well developed. In the past, most environmental monitoring was *ad hoc* in nature, which in many cases met the needs of the business at the time. The increasing turbulence in the human resource environments, however, made it necessary to reassess the basic approach to carrying out this responsibility. Two examples of reorganization at the corporate level described in the last section, illustrate the evolution that is taking place in this area.

Environmental analysis done by the human resource function is examined in the next section under the following headings: the external environment, the internal environment, and the role of the human resource executive.

The External Environment

Broadly speaking, the external human resource environment can be divided into four segments: social, political, technological and economic. Trends and developments in each of these areas, both domestically and internationally, must be monitored in a systematic manner.

Social trends include a wide variety of attitudes towards work in the context of lifestyles, towards the role and authority of institutions in society including business institutions, and towards collectivism as opposed to individualism. Some of these social trends address the basic concept of work and its role in society. Another aspect of social trends relates to changes in the demographic characteristics of the population and the work force. A number of these were discussed in Chapter I and include the aging of the work force, the increased percentage of women in the labour force, as well as growth in the number of part-time workers. Similar shifts in societal issues in many instances will lead to legislated government intervention.

It is important to be aware of social trends on a global as well as a domestic basis. Trends which emerge in one country, or in one part of the world, often show up in other countries at a later date. This, of course, is essential for organizations with multinational operations.

Political trends and issues can be analyzed at two levels. First, there are the more basic trends in political philosophy both domestically and internationally. A shift to the left of the political spectrum may result in changes in work place legislation or alter investment and hence employment decisions. A shift to the political "right" may have the opposite effect. Possible changes in political philosophy and their likely impact on the organization need to be assessed.

The analysis of the political environment at the second level would focus, in large part, on government policy and legislation in a wide variety of areas that have an impact on human resources. This goes all the way from federal trade policy affecting tariffs and quotas, which has an impact on both short- and long-term employment in an industry, to legislation in areas such as discrimination in the work place, health and safety, collective bargaining, pensions, plant closures, etc. In recent years, governments have placed increased attention on various aspects of legislation in the work place. This is likely to continue.

An analysis of *technological trends* includes changes in the technology of the business and its impact on human resources. Technological changes also include those that result from domestic and international competitive pressures or shifts in consumer preferences.

The analysis of *economic trends* focuses on the performance of the economy and is an area that, in many organizations, receives the greatest amount of attention. Employment levels are closely related to overall economic performance. In addition to the importance of the short-term economic trends on the organization and its human resources, economic monitoring also includes an examination of long-term trends. These would include areas such as manpower supply and demand in the long term and the implications of rising inflation on wage and salary expectations.

The examples presented above are not meant to be exhaustive, but rather illustrative of the broad scope of external environmental issues that may impinge on the organization's human resources.

Some Approaches to External Monitoring

There are a variety of approaches to monitoring the human resource external environment ranging from structured and sophisticated to unstructured and informal. Two examples of sophisticated approaches are political risk analysis and media content analysis. Political risk analysis assesses, in quantitative and qualitative terms, the risks involved in doing business in various countries of the world and provides a good basis for making major investment decisions, which have obvious human resource implications. Media content analysis attempts to monitor trends and issues in a society by recording, in a scientific fashion, the number of references made to a particular issue in the media, primarily newspapers. The rationale is that many trends and issues first gain attention in newspapers. Thus, analysis of these events gauges their importance.

Some organizations have devoted considerable resources to what is referred to as socio-political analysis, which is a disciplined and systematic approach designed to assist in forecasting the impact of significant external developments on company policies. Techniques involved include public opinion research, content analysis of the media, analysis of legislative issues and trends, special surveys, vulnerability analysis, etc.

An example is presented in Appendix V demonstrating how one organization has approached the environmental analysis part of the human resource strategic planning process. The human resource group is asked to undertake an external environmental analysis of trends in the following four areas: economic, technological, political, and social/cultural. The company's strategic objectives for the next five years are used as a guide for the analysis. Trends in each area are identified and analyzed according to the probable impact on the company and on human resource policies and programs.

A final and perhaps the most important monitoring "technique" is the involvement of human resource executives in activities outside the organization. This activity must be seen as an integral part of the human resource manager's job. This topic is discussed in more detail later in this chapter.

The Internal Environment

As described by one participant:

In many instances, an organization's internal population is a representation of society. Proper sensing of the internal environment can go a long way towards detecting trends in areas of interest and concern to employees.

Internal monitoring senses the attitudes, issues and concerns of employees at all levels of the organization and monitors the climate or morale of the organization and its component parts. In this regard, participants in the study agreed that an extremely important part of the internal monitoring process was management itself. The management process should provide ways of ensuring that managers are kept abreast of issues and concerns and that employees have ways of bringing areas of interest and concern to light.

A number of organizations have supplemented the normal management process with additional methods of identifying issues and trends. Such methods include the use of attitude surveys and programs where employees can anonymously obtain answers to questions. The case example described in Appendix W is from an organization that employs both approaches to monitoring — the ongoing management process and supplementary techniques.

The Role of the Human Resource Executive

The human resource executive and his staff have an important responsibility to perform in providing leadership for both internal and external environmental monitoring of issues related to human resources. The techniques and approaches described in the two previous sections of this chapter can provide the human resource executive with considerable environmental information. But this is only a part of the task. The human resource functional manager must also interact with both the internal and external environments. He must have effective means for "taking the pulse" of various parts of the organization, and his success in this regard will depend on how well his activities are integrated into the organization. This topic was discussed in Chapter V (Organizational Linkages) where it was concluded that human resource executives must be well linked with other parts of the organization.

The human resource executive must also develop effective means for keeping abreast of and interacting in the organization's external environments. One of the participants stated:

Our organization places very high value on external relations and contacts. We are strongly encouraged to build up a strong network of contacts outside the organization in our areas of expertise.

Said another:

In our organization, our senior executives feel we are adequately handling our responsibilities if we spend at least 50 per cent of our time in this endeavour. In many organizations, there must be a fundamental change in the perceptions of senior executives in this area.

Finally, another participant explained how the process evolved in his organization:

In 1975, I started to participate in activities outside our organization. I started to teach in the evening at a university school of business administration. I would discuss the things I was learning with the senior executives in our company. At the outset, they remarked that these things were interesting; however, they did not really see their relevance. However, over time their opinion changed and by 1979, I was asked to redefine my role in the company to incorporate the responsibility to build links with the various environments with which we deal. At the present time, outside interaction is the company norm for senior executives and it is not only actively encouraged, it is rewarded.

These quotations demonstrate that it is important for the senior human resource executive, as well as others in the function, to build effective relationships outside the organization.

The means of achieving this will vary among individuals. The following remark is instructive:

I have a number of different networks to which I belong. First, there is the industrial network. These are the associations in our particular industry. I attend a variety of trade shows to stay abreast of the technology of our business. We also have a group of human resource executives within the industry that meets periodically to discuss mutual problems. Second is the professional network. I belong to four different groups of human resource networks in Canada and elsewhere, and in these groups I keep abreast of developments in my field. Third is the academic network. I teach seminars periodically, and generally stay in touch with the academic community. We have a lot of university graduates and it is important for me to maintain good contacts. The fourth network relates to government. Government legislation is having such an impact on our organization that it is important for me to maintain good linkages both federally and provincially. At the provincial level I am a member of a government-sponsored committee looking at the impact of legislation in the work place. This may sound like a lot of outside activity, and, in fact, it is. However, when it is considered to be the number one priority in the statement of my responsibilities, then it is easy to see why I spend so much time at it.

This example, while perhaps not typical, was selected to indicate how some one individual views his responsibilities in this area. The amount of external involvement will depend on the individual preferences, work loads, organizational preferences, etc. The effort extended will likely be closely related to the value the organization places on external contacts.

The purpose of external monitoring is to keep informed about professional developments, to learn of the concerns and interests of others in similar positions, and to be aware of impending changes in the environment. These matters must be brought to the attention of the organization for appropriate action. The information gleaned from these activities is also useful to others in the function. The following comment is instructive:

> There is a need for the human resource executive to bring back into the organization, particularly to his functional subordinates, insights and directions gained from the environmental monitoring process. Without this there will be a tendency for middle and lower level human resource professionals to be working in greater isolation from the outside world and from the shocks that will come from it.

Influencing the Environment

For what appears to be a growing number of human resource executives, their role goes beyond that of monitoring the environment. In the words of one of the participants:

> My objective is to go beyond merely sensing and interpreting the impact of what is taking place outside the organization. It is equally important to participate in and influence the environment.

> Last year we had 36 legislative bills that impinged in one way or another on the management of our business. We would not be discharging our responsibilities if we did not attempt, in a very legitimate way, to influence the environment.

> To me the question is not whether business will attempt to influence potential outcomes, but whether it will be done overtly or covertly.

Organizations, and indeed individuals, will differ with respect to the importance they attach to the task of interacting with and influencing the external environments. In terms of influencing the various environments, one participant offered the following advice:

> It is fundamental that organizations not get involved in this area without explicit and clearly understood guidelines.

Some Observations

A number of observations can be made regarding the monitoring of the organization's human resource environments from the experience of participants in this study:

- Monitoring the external and internal environments must be explicitly recognized as an important responsibility of the human resource function and a process should be put in place to ensure that this monitoring is done.

- Monitoring includes issue identification, analysis of the potential impact of the issues on the organization, and possible short- and long-term responses. Further, there must be effective mechanisms for ensuring that these issues are assimilated into the decision-making processes of the organization.

- Developing action plans with respect to establishing and maintaining external contacts is an important function of the senior human resource executive, as well as other members of his staff.

Conclusion

Organizations operate in a complex and ever changing environment. The ability of an organization to adapt to its environments over time will have a major impact on its viability in the long run. Environmental analysis is thus an essential requirement for all organizations and must be a fundamental part of the management process. Senior line and functional managers have an important role to play in this regard. They must undertake effective monitoring of the organization's internal and external environments and take action in those areas that have a potential impact on the organization or a particular part of it. Each function of the organization including the human resource function has a responsibility to do this.

Assessing the organization's environments is not the final point in a sequence of events. Rather, it completes a cycle that began with the definition of corporate purpose and continued through strategic planning, organizational linkages, the role of the office of the chief executive officer, the line manager's responsibility for human resource management, and initiatives in the area of human resources.

Appendix A — Examples of Written Statements of Corporate Purpose — Organization 5 and Organization 2

This Appendix contains two examples of written statements of corporate purpose from Organizations 5 and 2.

Organization 5

This organization published an eight-page bilingual document in 1972 entitled *A Statement of Corporate Philosophy*, which contained the following introduction:

> When a corporation like ABC becomes large and operates in diverse business environments, the development of a written statement of corporate philosopy, and the distribution of that statement among its management personnel, takes on special significance and importance.

> Such a statement serves as an internal guideline to help management better understand the goals of the ABC organization and the management responsibilities associated with achieving those goals.

> Externally, it may serve a useful purpose to acquaint appropriate groups and individuals with the organization's operating and management philosophy.

> The corporate philosophy is not only an expression of the character and personality of the organization, it is, as well, a definition of the common goals that unify us despite the diversity of our business interests. Most important, it is a benchmark by which we may judge ourselves in the management of our vital resources.

> We also look upon our corporate philosophy as a living document that will undergo change as the needs and character of the corporation change as inevitably they will in time.

Following this introduction, the document states that the corporate philosophy has been developed to:

- describe how the organization will seek to manage and enhance its three principal resources: its people, its corporate reputation, and its financial and physical resources,

- contribute towards the development of distinctive corporate characteristics that will serve to distinguish the organization from other business enterprises,

- provide broad guidance to corporate, group and division management with respect to the establishment of these objectives and the measurement of performance.

The organization's corporate philosophy is divided into three parts (one for each of the three resources): people, corporate reputation, and financial and physical resources. Each part contains a general introductory statement, a description of how the resource will be managed and measures of success in managing the resource. The three introductory statements are presented below:

Part I — People[1]

The organization will be managed in such a way as to generate a climate of opportunity and challenge for each employee within which the individual can most effectively contribute to the fulfilment of his goals and those of the organization.

Part II — Corporate Reputation

It is recognized that the long-term success of the organization depends on the awareness and acceptance by its public of its role and progress as a business enterprise and, accordingly, that all components of the organization must ensure that these affairs are conducted in a manner compatible with the social, political and cultural environment in which each operates.

Part III — Financial and Physical Resources

The financial and physical resources of the organization will be managed in such a way as to enhance and protect shareholders' investments and to ensure the profitable perpetuation of the organization.

Organization 2

This organization issued a corporate philosophy document entitled, *Purpose, Objectives and Policy* in 1978. The document, which was published in 11 languages, contained the following introduction from the chairman and chief executive officer:

---

[1] The complete description of Part I is contained in Appendix B.

This statement of the Company's Purpose, Objectives and Policies is for distribution to employees in all countries to strengthen their awareness of the basic general principles and policies that have guided the conduct of the company business over the years. As a result of the consultation and participation of approximately 200 company managers in all geographic areas, the important task of presenting these principles as an agreed written document has been realized.

The statement is also being distributed to shareholders, and is available to members of interested groups and the general public on an unrestricted basis in all areas in which the Company is located.

It is not possible to prescribe specific responses to every industrial and social problem that will arise in a widespread international enterprise.

I have confidence, however, that the publication of this statement, and the continuing efforts of personnel to meet these standards, will enable the Company to continue to merit public understanding and trust.

Following an introductory section, and a section describing the company, the document was divided into three sections: corporate purpose, corporate objectives, and corporate policies. These three sections appear below in their entirety.

Corporate Purpose

The corporate purpose is to utilize profitably the risk voluntarily invested by the shareholders as a financial base to create productive facilities, employment and skills devoted to the production and distribution of the company's products to the public on an international scale. This purpose is based on the following convictions:

1. that the company's products possess superior properties for a large number of uses, is derived from raw materials that are abundant and, by combining lightness in weight and ease of recycling, incorporate qualities of energy conservation superior to many other materials;

2. that responsible, competitive, private enterprise is the most efficient system for producing and making products available to the public at large. We believe that this role is complementary to the responsibility of governments to develop their own priorities and goals, to set legal and taxation frameworks for corporate enterprises within their jurisdictions and thus to share in the economic benefits of industrialization;

3. that partnerships with national and local governments are on occasion appropriate, provided that our business objectives and their development aspirations are compatible.

Corporate Objectives

Recognizing that the conduct and effectiveness of an organization is highly dependent upon the quality of the people who comprise it, the company's ability to fulfil its purpose and to serve the following interdependent objectives is seen to require a complement of able employees who place a high value not only on the interest of the Company but also on the interests of other individuals and entities with whom they relate both inside and outside the company. These objectives are:

1. to operate at a level of profitability that will ensure the long-term economic viability of the Company by providing a return on the shareholders' investment, which compares favourably with other industries of similar capital intensity and risk and will enable the company to attract capital adequate to support its growth,

2. to maintain an organization of able and committed individuals in the many countries in which we operate and to provide opportunities for growth and advancement both nationally and internationally,

3. to strive for a level of operating, technical and marketing excellence that will ensure a strong competitive position in the various markets that we serve,

4. to recognize and seek to balance the interests of our shareholders, employees, customers, suppliers, governments and the public at large, while achieving the company's business objectives, taking into account the differing social, economic and environmental aspirations of the countries and communities in which we operate,

5. to maintain high standards of integrity in the conduct of all phases of our business.

Corporate Policies

In the pursuit of our objectives and respecting the laws, regulations, prevailing customs and practices in each of the countries in which we operate, we have adopted the following policies:

1. (a) to promote increased employee understanding of all aspects of their work and the recognition of how this work relates to the success of the enterprise,

    (b) to be alert to the attitudes and views of all employees,

(c) to employ and develop, to the greatest extent practicable, nationals in the countries where we operate,

(d) to provide opportunities for personal development and advancement to all with the required ability, ambition and integrity, in order to meet needs both in the local company and other companies within the corporate organization,

(e) to promote high standards of safety and occupational health,

(f) to provide wages, salaries and benefits that are fair and competitive in the relevant national or local contexts,

(g) to deal in good faith with all employees and employee representatives,

2. to publish information regularly regarding the company and its subsidiary companies on a consolidated basis giving, through compehensive accounts and otherwise, a clear picture of the overall structure, activities and performance of the group of companies,

3. to establish appropriate quality standards for the products we supply and to support similar efforts by trade associations and governments,

4. to improve our competitive position through continuing research and development; to encourage and support innovation in appropriate fields in every country in which we operate; to disseminate relevant technology and know-how to all consolidated group companies, having due regard to the protection of industrial and intellectual property rights and the need to give proper recognition for such development and transfer,

5. to conduct transactions among members of the company on a fair and equitable commercial basis,

6. to take all practical steps to prevent or abate all forms of pollution that result from our operations and to minimize requirements for energy and other natural resources in our processes,

7. to refrain from offering or receiving improper payments and to ensure that all financial transactions are properly recorded in the books of account; that books of account and accounting procedures are supported and reinforced by a comprehensive system of internal controls; and that they are available for inspection by the directors and auditors of each unit,

8. to require that our directors, officers and other employees in a position of trust in the parent company and subsidiaries remain free of disclosures, commitments and relationships that involve a conflict of interest with the company,

9. to be guided by principles of non-discrimination, respect for human rights and individuals' freedoms, and to refrain from improper involvement in political activities in the conduct of its business in all countries,

10. to engage in foreign exchange dealings only to the extent necessary to conduct the business and to protect the company's interests with respect to foreseen needs in accordance with prudent practice, and not to engage in currency transactions for the sole purpose of speculative profit,

11. to act independently and in the company's own interest in all commercial situations affecting competitive conditions of trade and not to engage in practices that restrict competition.

Appendix B — Statement of Corporate Purpose — Human Resource Dimensions — Organization 5

This appendix contains the human resource portion of the corporate philosophy document entitled, *A Statement of Corporate Philosophy* for Organization 5. Other parts of the document were described in Appendix A.

Part I — People

The organization will be managed in such a way as to generate a climate of opportunity and challenge for each employee within which the individual can most effectively contribute to the fulfilment of his goals and those of the organization. This will be accomplished by:

1. having a clear understanding of the qualities of each employee including skills, knowledge, potential, aspirations and limitations;

2. fostering a clear understanding with each employee of his job, his accountabilities and the standard of performance expected of him;

3. setting standards of performance that challenge each employee and by ensuring that this performance is attained;

4. rewarding appropriately excellent employee performance in both material and non-material terms;

5. planning its manpower needs essential to the realization of the business plans;

6. providing employees throughout the organization with opportunities for promotion, and for developing their job knowledge, skills and satisfaction;

7. practising a form of management that allows decision-making authority to be as decentralized as is practical;

8. developing an attitude of mutual support among all personnel throughout the organization, characterized by a climate of open and frank communication by and between all levels of management;

9. being alert and receptive to new and productive developments in the field of human resources management.

The Measure of Success

Successful management of people will be reflected by the presence of highly motivated employees, the ability to attract and hold people with above average performance records, and the availability of manpower necessary to achieve the goals of the organization.

Appendix C — Statement of Management System and Corporate Philosophy — Organization 10

This appendix contains the introduction to an internal management document that describes the company's management system. The appendix also includes another document entitled *A Statement of Corporate Philosophy*, which is made available to all employees and others who have a stake in the company.

1. A Statement of Management System

Corporate Environment and Philosophy

The environment in which the Company's mission is to be achieved must provide a balance between the controls necessary for efficient and effective operation of the Company and the freedom and scope provided to employees to permit them to show initiative and to realize their personal ambitions and goals. The Company has developed a group of management processes that provide this balance and are flexible enough to meet changing circumstances. This set of processes constitutes the management system.

The Company's management system is based on the belief that people can be trusted and given the opportunity will act in a responsible manner. The system encourages self-direction and assumes that each individual is capable of making decisions within the defined scope of responsibility of the position occupied. At the same time, standards of performance will be set at a high level and individuals will be held accountable for achieving approved goals.

In order for the system to operate effectively, open communication channels and prompt, objective communication of all information, both favourable and unfavourable, are required.

These requirements of trust, mutal respect, objectivity and open communication are concepts that cannot be measured or legislated, and must be accepted and encouraged as fundamental to the Company's practices. Inconsistencies must be continually challenged at all levels. The selection of managers will reflect and reinforce this philosophy.

The Company's Management Concept

The Company is a Management Company (as distinct from other forms such as a holding company or a financial conglomerate). Our definition of a Management Company is:

An industrial enterprise that contains a corporate management group having sufficient experience and current knowledge of each component business who are able to and will

(a) establish corporate strategies

(b) approve, cause changes in, and monitor objectives and policies of component businesses

(c) allocate resources to component businesses resulting in optimization of corporate performance.

The basic philosophy behind the Management Company concept is:

decentralized management with corporate strategic direction and control, and the provision of appropriate expert services.

This means that policy setting is centralized in the corporate management and operating freedom is exercised in each business.

2. A Statement of Corporate Philosophy

Philosophy

At XYZ, we believe it is our responsibility to contribute to the well-being of the economies and communities of which we are a part, and to ensure a prosperous future for the enterprise. Profits and growth are essential to fulfil this responsibility.

We will achieve our goals by producing high quality products and services, by providing rewarding and challenging opportunities for economic and personal growth for the people who work at XYZ, and by protecting the environment.

We will conduct our affairs with integrity, and respect the dignity and inherent rights of all people.

This philosophy will guide the corporation and will be the standard against which we test our activities. It will be prevalent in all relationships.

People

We believe people are important. We recognize the necessity of promoting the self-fulfilment and well-being of employees, as well as continuing concern for our retirees. We also recognize that we have expectations of our people that should be stated explicitly.

In continuing to create a good place in which to work, XYZ will provide:

● meaningful work with the opportunity for personal development and individual achievement,

- a safe, healthy working environment,

- a climate that encourages high quality standards and fosters participation, delegation of authority, innovation and open two-way communication,

- an evaluation system that communicates recognition of performance based on clearly defined duties, responsibilities and expectations.

A major determinant of personal success is the quality of an individual's performance. XYZ will expect:

- performance that produces high-level results and acceptance of accountability for performance,

- participation in the process of constructive change through open and frank communication,

- people to conduct themselves with integrity in the discharge of their job responsibilities,

- individuals to recognize that they must take personal initiative if they wish to achieve self-development and self-improvement,

- each individual to recognize and accept personal responsibility for safety for the individual, for co-workers and the public.

Environment

At XYZ, we are vitally concerned not only with the health and welfare of our employees but also with the well-being of those who buy and use XYZ products, and with the communities in which we operate.

We believe we have a responsibility to ensure that harm is not caused by any substances used in or derived from XYZ processes and products.

Customers

The success of our customers and ourselves is interdependent. Our mutual well-being is best achieved through the establishment of long-lasting business relationships. To fulfil this goal, XYZ will continue to provide a dependable source of safe, reliable, quality products at fair prices along with a high standard of technical and commercial service.

Further, we believe that our customers will benefit from our commitment to innovation. We will aggressively strive to be a technological leader in all fields of business, to seek opportunities to broaden our technical base, and to encourage innovation in all aspects of our operations.

Suppliers

Our dealings with our suppliers will be fair and will be based on a desire for continuing business relationships. Consistent with this, we will stress cost, quality and service.

Shareholders

We will provide our shareholders with a return on their investment at least equal to that which can be obtained by investing elsewhere at equal risk. Our responsibility to our shareholders is to optimize their financial return over time in order to maximize and protect the value of their investment.

Unions

XYZ will accept, without prejudice, the decision of employees on matters pertaining to union membership and representation. Where a group of employees is lawfully represented by a union, XYZ will strive to build a company-union relationship based upon mutual trust and respect.

Communities

XYZ will participate in relevant public issues and will make appropriate contributions to the economic and social development of the communities in which we operate. The company will take a responsible role in making each community a better place in which to live and work. We will place the highest priority on our commitment to a clean, safe environment.

We encourage and support the active participation of our people in their communities.

Governments

We recognize the need to establish and maintain sound relationships with all levels of government. We will deal in a forthright manner with local, regional and national governments in all countries in which we do business. We will speak out on those issues where our knowledge will assist governments in making informed decisions.

Appendix D — Organizational Purpose — Observations on the Process — Organization 2

The chief executive officer of Organization 2's largest subsidiary, who is also a director of the parent company, was highly involved with the process of developing the document on organizational purpose for the company. The following summarizes his observations of the process some two years after the document had been published.

1. The Importance of the Process

The process of formulating our corporate philosophy was extremely important for us. It helped us respond to a number of needs, which were being expressed from managers throughout the organization.

Managers in various parts of the world-wide organization needed to know where we stood on a variety of matters including our ownership positions in foreign countries, development of nationals, etc. They asked top management to give them guidance on where the company stood on these and other matters. As well, foreign governments and shareholder groups asked us to clarify similar concerns.

As a result of this process, the company became much more aware of its environment. We are a resource-based company and it is very important for us to be concerned with and responsive to our environment.

Equally important was the fact that the process was the starting point of a long-term project that examined our strategic direction. Once we clarified our philosophy, we were able to deal more effectively with the strategic direction of the business. This work has now been completed.

2. The Philosophy in Practice

We certainly do not refer to our corporate philosophy on a daily basis; however, I can say that we refer to it regularly. For example, it is referred to in our strategic and operational plan to ensure that our strategies reflect all major areas of our corporate philosophy. In this sense, it acts as a check to ensure that we are paying attention to all the things we say we should.

The corporate philosophy has had a particular impact on how we think about two areas in particular — employee and industrial relations, and environmental concerns. Articulating our beliefs and values about these areas has helped us greatly in formulating strategies and programs, and in evaluating our performance in these areas.

Finally, to ensure that our company abides by the statement of corporate philosophy, I have had it framed and put on my office wall. This serves as a useful reminder that we must practise what we preach.

3. On Human Resource Dimensions

Organizations are all about people. It is very important to place the company where it fits in its environment. This is the reason we wrote the introductory statement in our document. In a mixed economy, managers should understand where they fit in society. Once this is clear, we could then describe our values and beliefs about our employees throughout the world.

4. Relating Philosophy to Behaviour

It is a continuous struggle to practise what you espouse. We continually strive to live up to the standards we establish, and think the process we went through will be beneficial. Thus, inside the organization, we feel we are on the right track. It is more difficult with external groups (governments, shareholders, etc.). Here, the problem of how the company's behaviour is perceived by external groups is extremely difficult to deal with.

If you are going to expose the document outside the company, it should be done after a period of time. Practise it inside first and then, when you feel confident, you can tell others to judge us on our principles. External exposure, however, is not nearly as important as internal exposure.

5. Some Cautions

- There are two traps you can fall into. First, once the formal documentation is completed, you cannot say that you have finished the work. Second, if you are not careful, the written expression can be treated too mechanistically — "I quote the text to you, and you to me." You have to watch for these two traps.

- The conciseness of the statements of corporate philosophy can make them seem simplistic. For example, in the area of safety, perfection must be the goal. These statements describe ideal conditions that are unattainable, and yet, one has to continue to strive towards the ideal.

- A simplistic statement can lead to criticism from labour unions or other groups if it falls short of your ideal. In spite of this, I feel it is important for people to see that you are continually striving towards the company's ideal.

  The unions do not recognize our statement and do not feel bound by it. In many cases, we still end up in a conflict situation, and thus the document does not seem to have much influence. Again, I feel that in the long run it will help both the unions and management. It is a testing ground to show unions that we can live up to our ideals.

  It is also important that we continually strive for perfection in the area of work place legislation, i.e., health and safety.

- There can be a feeling of intense disappointment after the formal part of the process has been completed because of the tendency of the statements to be "motherhood" in nature. This does not bother me, however, because even "motherhood" statements in many organizations can be poorly thought out.

- It is hard to get an understanding of the philosophy throughout the organization. I refer to it continually, but in subtle ways. For example, it is referred to at foremen meetings when a particular issue is being discussed.

6. The Wider Use of Statements of Corporate Philosophy

Very few organizations in Canada seem to have gone through this process compared to the United States and elsewhere. It seems that more of the international companies have prepared statements of corporate philosophy as more and more sensitive issues are encountered.

Appendix E — Corporate Strategic Human Resource Guidelines — Organization 2

The senior human resource executive in this organization described his insights into the five items making up the corporate strategic human resource guidelines shown in Exhibit 1 of Chapter III. The item numbers below correspond to the numbers in Exhibit 1.

Item 1: This statement is important because succession planning in the past had been quite informal. This statement makes it clear that the process will be better structured and a part of strategic planning. This has become a very important part of overall management strategy.

Item 2: This statement is significant because the corporate organization is recognizing that, in today's world, the attitudes and aspirations of all employees are becoming an increasingly important concern.

Item 3: Historically, the corporate organization always encouraged the subsidiary companies to promote the area of health and safety, but there has never been a strong program or follow-up from the centre. This statement provides a much stronger role for the corporate organization. Now, each unit will be expected to mount a health and safety program, which will be included in the organization's strategic and operational plans.

Item 4: Over the course of the last five years, we were forced to close down or divest some of our operations. A number of things were done to soften the impact of these changes on our employees. This statement is a more formal recognition that in today's world the organization has to be doing more in this regard.

Item 5: This last strategic thrust is important. Ten years ago we established business units with decentralized decision making. These business units were given economic yardsticks against which to measure performance. Over time this led to a number of organizational negatives. It tended to make people preoccupied with their own part of the organization. It was clear that there had to be a more co-ordinated effort from the centre to take broader concerns into account. To this end, we developed a concept of "organizational transparency," which is described in Item 5.

In the past, country general managers did not welcome or take the initiative to involve parts of the organization outside their unit whether they be finance, technology or personnel. The concept of organizational transparency makes it legitimate for a part of the corporate organization (personnel for example) to come in and work with the business unit. It was important for the country general managers to understand that there were skills at the centre (head office), that they were not self-sufficient, and that they could and should make use of resources from other countries as well as the corporate staff.

The executive vice president with the largest regional line responsibility recently summarized his philosophy on this subject as follows: "I am not satisfied with getting information only from people who report to me. I am going to rely heavily on corporate staff, and others, to help me to get my job done." He has done a lot to bring down barriers.

Appendix F — Diagram Relating Corporate and Human Resource Planning Processes — Organization 3

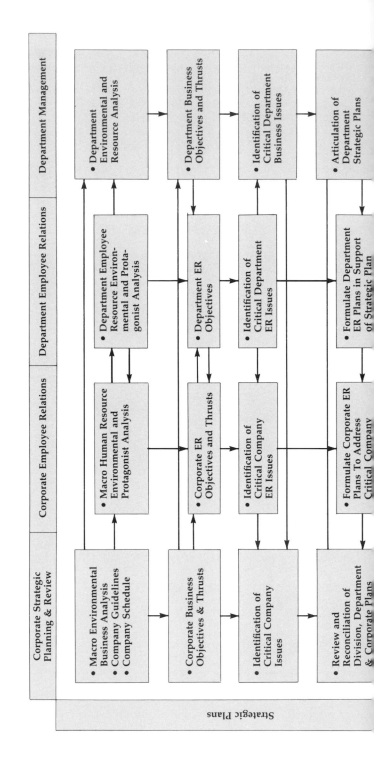

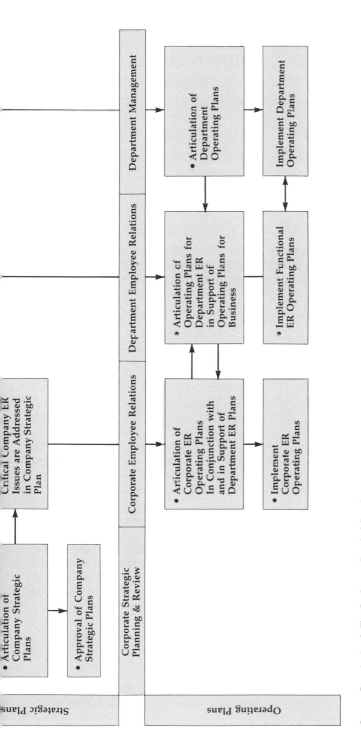

Source: Organization 3; The Conference Board of Canada.

Appendix G — Human Resource Component of a Strategic Plan — Organization 10

This appendix contains the portion of the 1980 corporate strategic plan for Organization 10, which dealt with human resources. It contains an environmental analysis and a number of key planning assumptions and implications.

1980 Strategic Plan — Human Resource Component

Environmental Analysis

The fundamental business environment characteristics of high inflation, high unemployment, and modest real growth will have significant implications for human resource cost, availability, and management. Areas of significant concern in the human resource environment are the maintenance of productivity and adaptations to change in general attitudes of people towards work, working conditions, and lifestyles.

Productivity will tend to be reduced through a number of factors. Acceptable working conditions and work environment will be increasingly defined by legislation. Europe leads in this area, but the *Occupational Safety and Health Administration Act* in the United States is also significant. These changes will be restrictive. There are clear trends developing towards fewer hours worked per year, resistance to shift work and resistance to overtime (or compulsory compensation with time off). The current relatively high wage escalation rates will continue, and the cost of many benefit items will go up. A specific example is the cost of pensions, indexing provisions, and early retirement options. Labour unrest and sporadic work stoppages will continue, particularly in European countries. (Reference to actual countries deleted). Country A and Country B have unhealthy labour climates while unrest in Country C tends to be more cyclical and related to political events. In Country D, a strained and "secretive" attitude by management has been generated due to work councils, and this in turn reduces work effectiveness.

In addition, the company as an international corporation will face hostility in operations where foreign ownership is perceived as a threat. There will also be increasing costs associated with international activities, since people will be less ready to transfer to other locations or countries, and high differentials will be needed to maintain expatriated employees.

Given the characteristics of the business environment over the plan period, the company should have no problem attracting and retaining required manpower as current plans require only marginal manpower increases. The environment, however, does dictate changes in personnel policies, compensation plans, and management leadership styles, with a fundamental focus given to productivity improvement. Senior management succession must also be addressed throughout the planning period.

Key Planning Assumptions (Partial)

- Major demographic trends will lead to an older population and slower growth in the labour force through the 1980s.

- The government will increase its use of the corporate sector as an instrument of economic and social policy, with added work place legislation.

- Worker attitudes, particularly union activities, may become increasingly militant. For example:
    — increased hostility toward multinational corporations,
    — trend to work councils and co-determination in running of companies.

- High labour costs with significant increases in non-wage benefits will continue.

- Unionization of white collar workers and increased labour participation in management decision-making will continue.

- Emphasis on improving productivity essential to offset the general cost squeeze and the pressure on profit margins will increase.

Key Implications (Partial)

- Personnel policies, compensation plans, and management leadership styles will need to reflect trends such as increased worker participation, changing age mix, and minority group pressures (North America).

- Compensation packages will become more complex and more costly (e.g., portable pensions, health benefits, career development, etc.).

Appendix H — Human Resource Objectives and the Business Planning Process — An Example — Organization 7

This example describes the method used to define human resource objectives at the corporate and subsidiary levels in Organization 7 as part of the business planning process. Also shown is how this process relates to defining the responsibilities of individual managers.

While this example focuses on responsibilities and accountabilities in the short term (the operating plan), it is necessary to set the stage by reviewing briefly the strategic planning process.

Corporate Level

The strategic objectives of the corporation are developed by the Policy Committee and are communicated to subsidiaries through a series of meetings as well as by formal documentation. The corporate strategic objectives include a human resource component.

Using these strategic objectives, each business unit prepares a five-year business plan. The five-year plan, which includes the coming year, becomes the operating plan for the business unit. These plans are reviewed at the corporate level and approved. From the operating plans of all the business units emerges the operating plan for the corporation for the next year (and four additional years).

The operating plan for the corporation also has an explicit human resource component, which is in two parts: first, a number of key corporate human resource projects that will be accomplished in the coming year, and second, a series of key indicators on the human resource areas. These 22 indicators in their present state of development, shown in the accompanying table, are reported on a total corporate basis each quarter and used primarily to analyze trends. The indicators are guidelines and are interpreted with care. It will take some time before it can be determined how effective an indicator the performance indexes (the last item in the accompanying Table) are.

Subsidiary Level

Each subsidiary has a five-year business plan. The structure of the subsidiary's operating plan resembles that of the corporate operating plan and includes a human resource component containing the two sections described above. Each subsidiary establishes

Annual Corporate Business Plan
Human Resource Component — Key Data
Organization 7

	Actual Forecast		Business Plan				
	1980	1981	1982	1983	1984	1985	1986

EMPLOYEES (DEC. 31)
Managers (K.W.s)[1]
Professionals (K.W.)
Other K.W.s
Other Employees
Total Employees

RATIOS
K.W.s: Total Employees
Non-Managers: Managers
Non-Managers: First
  Line Managers

ATTRITION
% Loss K.W.s
% Loss Total Employees
Separation Costs $M

GROWTH & REPLACEMENT (G & R)
% K.W.s
% Total Employees
G & R Costs $M

COMPENSATION COSTS % SALES
Managers (K.W.s)
Professionals (K.W.)
Other K.W.s
Total Employees

PERFORMANCE INDICES
Earnings/Compen-
  sation (1978 = 100)
Managers (K.W.)
Professionals (K.W.)
Other K.W.s
Total Employees

---

[1] K.W. denotes "knowledge workers", a term used to describe those who are employed in positions that require managerial, professional and technical competence, and which are critical to the present and future performance of the organization.

129

human resource indexes in 22 key areas and reports on them on a quarterly basis.

Individual Manager Level

The subsidiary's operating plans are a consolidation of individual departmental operating plans. The key objectives of the departmental plans are, in fact, the major objective of the managers, who are assigned specific responsibilities. Emphasis is placed on the individual's role and responsibility for achieving business objectives through the company's "Managing for Achievement" process.

Implementing Plans and Control

Each subsidiary submits quarterly human resource data relative to key indexes established in its operating plan (e.g., number and types of employees, loss and hiring rates and associated costs, compensation costs and indexes, productivity performance indexes, etc.).

These data are consolidated into a Human Resource Quarterly Key Indicator report to the Policy Committee. This report includes a corporate perspective as well as a section on each subsidiary. Overall trends and problem areas are identified.

The vice president, human resources, for each of the subsidiaries prepares a similar report for the president of the subsidiary. The quarterly reports provide the basic input to a series of quarterly performance review meetings where issues are discussed and corrective action taken.

The individual manager's performance is evaluated annually through a Management Evaluation and Development Review process, which is results oriented.

Appendix I — Defining the Profile of Future Managers — An Example — Organization 10

The XYZ Company has a management forum known as the Management Council. This Council serves as an assembly for managers and senior executives, reinforces functional and line management relationships, provides input to corporate plans and policies, communicates strategic issues to and from the Management Committee (the senior management council of the organization), and provides an opportunity for group interaction on issues common to XYZ's business.

Currently, the membership on the Management Council comprises approximately 25 senior executives and meets three to four times a year. Council meetings, which are usually held over a four-day period, tend to be heavily task-oriented, and the format usually consists of a session with the entire group along with smaller workshops that delve into problem areas and report to the members.

In late 1979, the Management Council determined that its attention would focus on the company's managerial requirements in the 1980s with particular reference to the latter half of the decade, specifically, on a qualitative profile of future XYZ managers. Outside facilitators were hired to work with the Management Council to develop this profile.

The project explored the significance of a rapidly changing environment for the actual and potential role of management, and discussed the broader issues of modern society, their effect on the management function in general, and on the management of XYZ in particular. The project was designed to enable executives to play an active role in exploring what was felt would be the key characteristics of the XYZ manager in the late 1980s.

At the June 1980 meeting of the Management Council, the chief executive officer outlined his thoughts on the project.

> In my judgment, our limiting resource is now the capacity of our managerial and professional resources. This project will have a significant payoff in that we will develop a profile or set of profiles of the manager of the future, specifically the 1985–90 period. These profiles will help to develop training programs designed to enable present managers to handle the changing managerial requirements and to prepare them for additional managerial responsibilities. Of equal importance will be the help provided in the selection and development of new managers. Both upgrading the existing pool of talent and creating an enlarged pool are required to exploit XYZ's potential for profitable growth.

The members also decided to form a subcommittee of the Management Council to formulate recommendations for a managerial profile of the future, based on the findings of the Council up to that point. The subcommittee met several times throughout the fall and winter of 1980 to prepare the profile, which was presented to, and approved by, the Management Council at their February 1981 meeting.

Members of the Council developed a strong sense of ownership and commitment to both the profile, and to the updated statement of corporate philosophy that was reviewed as part of the project.[1] The profile was also integrated into the regular annual manpower planning process of the company. The profile of the XYZ Manager of the 1980s is presented below and is preceded by a preamble.

Preamble
Criteria for the XYZ — Manager of the Eighties

The criteria, considered an essential attribute of the XYZ manager for the '80s, should be viewed as supplementary to that part of the XYZ *Statement of Corporate Philosophy* dealing with people. Thus, the XYZ manager of the '80s has an obligation, on the one hand, to provide the conditions specified in the philosophy as necessary for implementing the company's concern for people. On the other hand, he has an obligation through his behaviour to live up to the expectations XYZ has of its employees. There should be no inconsistencies between the corporate philosophy's statements about people and the definitions of the criteria.

It is not expected that every future XYZ manager will exhibit all the behavioural characteristics embodied in these criteria. The relative importance of the criteria will depend on the type of job (e.g., the characteristics of the risk-taker/entrepreneur are incompatible with the characteristics of the team player). Since no manager is likely to be strong in all of the behaviours specified, any one management team should contain a mix of individuals whose behaviour complements one another vis-à-vis these criteria.

Profile of the XYZ Manager of the Eighties

Team Player

A manager acts as a team player when he or she:

1. draws on the resources of others for assistance in problem solving and decision making,

2. assists colleagues in achieving their goals,

---

[1] The statement of corporate philosophy is referred to in Chapter III and is contained in Appendix C under the heading "A Statement of Corporate Philosophy."

3. shares with others, rather than taking from others, accountability for achieving the goals of the organization,

4. identifies in his or her actions with the goals of the larger organization — he or she says "we" not "I."

Leader — People Developer

A manager acts as a leader and people developer when he or she:

1. commands attention and respect (from superiors, peers, and subordinates),

2. generates a sense of purpose and direction in subordinates,

3. works with subordinates not only as a teacher but also as a coach,

4. creates an environment that stimulates people to make the most of their potentialities,

5. lives with the ambiguity of not being able to control all outcomes, and of not knowing at all times what his or her subordinates are doing.

Risk Taker — Entrepreneur

A manager acts as a risk taker and entrepreneur when he or she:[2]

1. moves ahead on a course of action in which he or she believes in, even when uncertain of the outcome,

2. is not merely comfortable working with probabilities rather than certainties, but is at his or her best when undertaking ventures with unpredictable outcomes,

3. acts purposefully and confidently in uncertain or unstructured situations,

4. believes that his or her own energy, conviction and skill can shape events and win the day (entrepreneurs are often "I" people rather than "we" people).

Effective Communicator

A manager is an effective communicator when he or she:

1. expresses himself or herself directly and unequivocally,

2. is responsive to the attitudes, needs and ideas of others,

---

[2] These behaviour statements are based on actual studies of successful entrepreneurs; however, individuals who fail as entrepreneurs could exhibit any one of these characteristics. Actual track record separates the successes from the failures.

3. leaves no doubt in others' minds as to how he or she feels and thinks on important issues,

4. is a good listener and observer.

Executor

A manager is an effective executor when he or she:

1. makes incisive decisions,

2. puts ideas into action and gets results,

3. resolves tough problems without wavering,

4. holds people accountable for meeting "stretch" objectives.

Conceptualizer

A manager demonstrates conceptual ability when he or she:

1. goes beyond the pragmatic or "doing" parts of the job — deals effectively with intangibles, as well as with tangibles,

2. integrates information — is able to create a broad, coherent picture out of diverse facts,

3. anticipates long-range implications of current activities,

4. generates ideas.

Environmentally Sensitive

A manager demonstrates environmental sensitivity when he or she:

1. puts aside personal inclinations to respond to external realities,

2. takes actions within the organization and anticipates actions from outside the organization,

3. communicates with individuals and groups in the larger environment (e.g., community agencies, government, labour) within which the organization functions,

4. co-operates with other organizations on problems whose resolution may be only partly within the manager's ability to solve and for whose existence the manager's organization may be only partly responsible.

Appendix J — Succession Planning Framework — An Example — Organization 1

This example contains some of the guidelines that this organization provides to managers to be used in the process of identifying senior management potential. The material is called *"A Guide for Use in the Assessment of Potential."*[1]

The material presented below is an example of an employee relations initiative designed to provide an instrument for the identification of leadership potential and to foster an understanding of the need for certain additional management skills in an environment of internal and external change.

A Guide for Use in the Assessment of Potential

- An old axiom says: "What a person has done is not a guarantee of what he or she can do in the future but it is the best measure available."

- The employee whose performance will be subjected to additional scrutiny will have a record of achievement in the company. This assessment is not so much concerned with those achievements that are a matter of record but with the more qualitative aspects of how they were won.

- The framework used asks that you think about the employee in four organizational settings:

  — as a professional,

  — in relation with people who report to him/her,

  — in relation with other units in the company,

  — in relations between the company and the external environment (to the extent of actual exposure).

- The listing of Managerial Capacities (see Item 1 below) is not intended as a check list of questions but should be used to guide your attention to those qualities and skills that have contributed to or detracted from performance *in a significant manner*.

---

[1] The evaluations that result from this process are subject to an ascending series of reviews as described in Appendix N. Appendix N shows the delegation of authority and responsibility for a number of senior levels of management. It illustrates that the responsibility for the identification of management potential, and its further development, should be widely pervasive in the organization. Appendix N is discussed in Chapter VIII.

Item 1

**Framework for Assessing Management Potential
Managerial Capacities**

Ability To Act

How has he demonstrated his effectiveness?

How does he execute plans and accomplish objectives, both on his own and with others?

How does he assess results?

How does he use resources?

What is the quality and quantity of the information he provides?

How does he influence people, and how is he influenced by them?

How does he deal with conflicts?

How do people react to him?

Forming Judgments

How does he explore opportunities and assess attendant risks?

How does he relate his immediate concerns to the broader interests of the company?

How does he arrange priorities?

How does he balance attention to short-term problems with attention to long-term strategies?

How does he use qualitative and quantitative data?

How does he deal with complexity and uncertainty?

How does he learn from experience?

As Head of a Unit

How does he co-operate?

How does he handle difficult issues?

How does he deal with crises?

How does he influence the climate in his unit?

How does he read and respond to trends?

How does he promote development?

What is the breadth of his outlook?

- The Summary Assessment of Manager Potential (see Item 2 below) is aimed at focusing your deliberations on areas of future concern for the company and *possibly* the individual — the latter depends on the extent to which the individual (and you) can constructively use the information.

Item 2
Framework for Assessing Management Potential
Summary Assessment of Management Potential

NAME:_____

WHAT ARE THE PRINCIPAL STRENGTHS?

HOW CAN THESE BEST BE USED IN THE COMPANY?

WHAT ARE THE PRINCIPAL DEFICIENCIES?

CAN/SHOULD THEY BE REMEDIED? (Education, training and/ or particular assignments?)

WHAT IS THE POTENTIAL? (Realistic assessment with experience and standard planning assumptions?)

NEXT ASSIGNMENT

ULTIMATE

PREPARED BY: _____ DATE: _____

Appendix K — Partial Position Description — Senior Executive — Organization 10

This appendix contains a partial position description of a senior operating vice president. The other parts of the description define the basic purpose of the position, the nature and scope of the responsibilities that are business specific, and key relationships with others, both internal and external. An attempt has been made to specify performance measures opposite each major responsibility.

Accountabilities/ Responsibilities	Performance Measures
1. Operate the business of the group to optimize short- and long-range terms on investment within agreed strategies. Ensure that this is accomplished with adherence to all corporate policies and practices.	Achievement of adequate return without any policy or practice deviations
2. Direct the development of the mission, strategy and role for the businesses, including expansion or shutdown of individual components. This could include some acquisition and divestment.	Acceptance of plan by CEO
3. Develop the annual and long-range operating and capital plans and budget for corporate approval, together with plans for accomplishing those budgets.	Soundness of plans and projections as judged by the President, with an agreed upon minimum number of surprises. Ability to predict and respond appropriately to changing external activities and the environment.
4. Co-operate and respond to appropriate corporate functional groups in their areas of functional activity; i.e. Research and Development, Finance and Administration, and Personnel.	Results measured by extent to which joint co-operation and actions produce effective standards of performance and successful implementation of Company's integrated management system.
5. Establish and maintain standards of technical and professional competence for all	Quality of leadership and selection, as demonstrated by effectiveness of such personnel.

subordinate line personnel and share responsibility with functional heads for ensuring the effective selection, performance assessment, and deployment of related staff throughout this group.

6. Provide for succession to this position by ensuring the personal development of subordinate managers within this group.

Long-term depth and strength sufficient to meet business and corporate needs, with a minimum of external recruiting

7. Stay informed and sensitive to the social, political, economic, technological and government environments where the company operates, and be responsive to changes affecting the business.

Soundness of predictions and ability to respond effectively to changing internal and external environments

Maintain a good public image of the business.

Effectiveness and perception of our role in industry

8. Assist the President, as directed, in managing the corporation for optimal results.

Value and extent of contribution

Appendix L — Human Resource Objectives — An Example — Organization 10

This organization has a highly-developed goal and objective-setting process, of which the main driving force behind its fulfilment is the chief executive officer. In addition to the long-range strategic plan for the corporation, the current-year operating goals include a specific section on human resources. Extensive energies are devoted to linking these corporate goals to human resource objectives for individual executives. This appendix shows how one of the 1979 corporate human resource goals was translated into an objective for a group vice president and his immediate subordinate. Note the follow-up procedures established to ensure adherence to the accomplishment of this goal.

Part I — The President's Goal

Goal 4: Develop career plans for identified high-potential individuals within the upper middle management group and continue progress against senior management manpower planning gaps.

> *Test:*
>
> Ensure approved growth plans for all high-potential individuals, and plans to close all senior management planning gaps are in place by Dec. 1979.
>
> *Operations:*
>
> 1. Continue progress against the identified high-priority manpower planning gaps and problems at the senior management level.
>
> 2. Each designated senior manager, assisted by corporate personnel, develops a manpower plan for his area of responsibility by June 1979.
>
> 3. Upper middle management gaps are identified and succession plans developed by Dec. 1979.

Part II — The Group Vice President's Goal

Goal 6: Complete development plans for identified high-potential individuals in the business, and plan for their implementation.

Tests:

(a) Career plans for all identified high-potential individuals are completed by April 30, 1979.

(b) At least 50 per cent of the identified individuals have moved one step along their career path in 1979.

Operations:

1. Confirm the high-potential list for business by January 31, 1979

Responsibility: ABC

2. Set goals for all direct subordinates to complete career plans for their high-potential employees by February 28, 1979

Responsibility: ABC

3. Review these plans at manpower planning meeting with direct subordinates and corporate personnel by March 15, 1979

Responsibility: ABC

4. Present these plans to president's council when scheduled by corporate personnel (after March 15, 1979)

Responsibility: ABC

Note: Based on current tests, effective implementation of the above will produce an effective plan to fill and back up all senior management positions in the business and contribute to the back-up for other senior positions in the Company.

Part III — Vice President's Goal

Goal 4: Develop career plans and progress for high-potential employees in middle management.

Test:

Career plans in place for all supervisors and class "O" personnel in location A by end of first quarter, 1979

Each Manager reporting to DE at January 1, 1979 has a significant change in job responsibility in place or firmly scheduled by December 31, 1979

Operations:

1. Implement organization career plans developed in 1978 by June 30, 1979

Responsibility: DE

2. Implement main features of the study of the business structure.

Responsibility: DE

3. Develop career plans for all supervisors and class "O" personnel with concurrence of DE and personnel function

Responsibility: FGH/IJK/LMN

4. Ensure appropriate development plans and individual growth objectives for all staff by March 31, 1979, and proceed to target condition by December 31, 1979

Responsibility: ALL

Appendix M — Individual Objectives and an Executive Performance Award Plan — Organization 2

This appendix describes the approach used by this company in setting corporate and key managers' objectives. It also describes how the review of accomplishment of objectives is tied in with the executive bonus plan.

Objective-Setting

1. By May of each year the Chief Executive Officer (C.E.O.) and other key officers in the head office draft suggested key objectives for the company for the coming year under five headings.

   Strategy
   Major projects
   Resources
   Organization
   Operations

2. These proposed objectives are distributed to all company officers (23), with a view to obtaining comments and suggestions by June.

3. In July the C.E.O., assisted by the three members of the C.E.O.'s office and three staff officers, decide what the key objectives for the next year will be.

   These objectives are then distributed to all company officers. Each officer is asked to select the specific objectives applicable to his area or function as key inputs to their local objective planning process. Personal objectives of the top 250 managers are prepared and approved by the appropriate managers before the start of the performance year.

4. In addition, there are processes at various levels of management for sharing of objectives. An example of this is a day-long meeting where all company officers in the head office (17) review their objectives so that a good understanding and provision for mutually interdependent objectives exists.

Performance Review

1. There are periodic reviews of progress throughout the performance year. Necessary objectives can be revised, although this is not frequently done.

2. At the end of the year, performance relative to objectives is measured and this determines the amount of the variable bonus. This bonus has two components, one based on overall company performance and the other on personal performance.

Appendix N — A Framework for the Delegation of Personnel Authority and Responsibility in the Line Organization — Organization 1

Level	Policies and Programs	Staff Planning	Individual Transactions	Transactions Affecting Groups of Employees — Incl. Collective Bargaining
President	• Approval of all Corporate policies and programs in those areas delegated by the Board of Directors. • Recommendations as to new or amended policies and programs for approval by the Board of Directors, as appropriate.	• Appraisal of Company's management manpower inventory. • Primary selection and development of canditates for Sr. Vice President, Vice President and General Manager positions. • Recommendations to the Board of Directors of candidates for election/appointment as Officers.*	• Excluding the election of Officers and transactions specifically requiring Board approval, initial approval of all personnel transactions relating to Sr. Vice Presidents and Vice Presidents, and of initial transactions relating to General Managers.*	• Discretion

* The President is a member of the Human Resources and Remuneration Committee to which the Board of Directors has delegated the authority to fix current compensation for officers and general managers; to recommend to the Board individual awards of deferred compensation and election or appointment of officers.

Sr. Vice Presidents

— Together with the President, the Senior Vice Presidents constitute the Senior Executive Group. In this mode, Senior Vice Presidents will advise and assist the President in the exercise of his authority and responsibility in senior staff planning, remuneration of senior staff issue identification, strategic responses and policy and program development.

— As Contact Officers, the Senior Vice Presidents have authority and responsibility as follows:

Level	Policies and Programs	Staff Planning	Individual Transactions	Transactions Affecting Groups of Employees — Incl. Collective Bargaining
		• To ensure an adequate succession inventory for senior jobs such as Plant Manager, Region Manager, Business Division Manager and like graded jobs in Corporate Functions. • To ensure the identification of candidates for general manager/vice president levels.	• Excluding those designated above, to approve all personnel transactions in salary Grade Y and to ensure they are consistent with staff planning. • To ensure that the development and rewarding of accepted senior candidates is consistent with Senior Staff plans.	• Within the Businesses or Corporate Functions for which he is the Contact Officer, to approve proposals involving significant changes in organization, manpower levels, working conditions and the pay of groups of employees, including those subject to collective bargaining. The President's agreement is required for proposals which might have wide corporate relevance.
Vice Presidents and General Managers	— As members of Human Resources Committees they contribute to the processes of policy review, issue identification, strategic responses and policy/program development for presentation to the Senior Executive Group. — As Heads of Businesses or Corporate Functions they assist and advise the Senior Vice President or Vice President as appropriate in all the above areas. They have authority and responsibility as follows: • To ensure the administration and evaluation of Corporate policies and programs within his area of accountability. • To stimulate the development, administration and evaluation of policies and programs which are of particular relevance to his Business.	• Appraisal of management manpower inventory within the Business or Function. • Approval of the identification and development of all candidates for managing, high level specialist jobs, other than those designated above.	• Approval of all personnel transactions up to and including jobs in Salary Grade X.	• Within the Business or Function is responsible: — for coordinating and formulating for Sr. Vice President's approval proposals regarding significant organizational change, manpower utilization and rationalization, working

conditions, and remuneration of groups of employees (including those subject to collective bargaining), and

— for generally directing the implementation and execution of approved proposals

ness and to ensure that they are not in conflict with the needs of Corporate integrity.

• Appraisal of manpower requirements within the Business or Function and the development of programs for rationalizing, utilizing and developing of employees at all levels other than those designated above.

NOTES: 1. The role of Human Resources in each of the above topic areas is

• The anticipation of needs, through diagnosis of external and internal conditions, which require Corporate or Business responses.

• The development of responsive policies and programs for approval by the appropriate level of management.

• The development of policy and program evaluation techniques.

• Assistance and advice to appropriate levels of management in the execution and evaluation of policies and programs.

• To provide staff work and other assistance in the operation of Human Resources Committees.

2. Individual Transactions and Transactions Affecting Groups of Employees refer to Employment and Transfers (Additions to Staff, Replacement Staff, Transfers Within and Out of Department, Salary Changes, Reclassification and Promotion, Salary Grade Determination, Job Titles, Leaves of Absence and Termination of Employment. All transactions should conform with statutory requirements and the exercise of authority is to be guided by Corporate policies and, where applicable, collective bargaining requirements.

Appendix 0 — Corporate Personnel Department
— Description of Main Functions
— Organization 2

This appendix contains a description of the five functions of the corporate personnel department for Organization 2.

1. Personnel and Organizational Planning and Development

This function is to ensure that:

I   The company will have a management group composed of both managers and staff specialists, well balanced in professional skills, international outlook, and experience.

Succession planning activities are:

- co-ordinated at top levels of the organization (corporate, region, area, country).
- supportive of organization planning efforts.

Planning for functional skills groups is co-ordinated, i.e., financial, raw materials.

II   Proper approaches, policies and systems to handle international transfer requirements will be maintained and developed. Emphasis will be placed on:

- proper follow-up during the assignment and re-integration into the home base.
- The maintenance of a central registry of all those on international assignments.

III   The staff and organizational requirements of new business strategies will be identified early, and action plans to meet them will be implemented.

IV   Instances of persistent organizational ineffectiveness or conflict will be identified and resolved.

2. Personnel Research and Planning

This function is concerned with long-term trends and planning to meet anticipated changes mainly in the field of employee relations. It seeks to ensure that the following areas are dealt with:

I   co-ordinating corporate and area studies on the impact of social, political, and economic trends on employee and industrial relations;

II   monitoring international institutional developments such as international unions, OECD, ILO, etc., which have an impact on employee and industrial relations;

III   developing an understanding by corporate and area management of key trends affecting employee relations, and by developing action plans that take these into account;

IV   developing and implementing approaches and methods to assure integration of personnel planning into business planning;

V   promoting a better exchange of information and co-ordinating the development of:

- the most effective approaches to employee relations and human resource management,

- programs to improve safety and health conditions at all locations.

3.   Group Compensation and Benefits

This function is concerned with:

I   development and application of total compensation practices for corporate executives;

II   integration of executive evaluation and compensation between the corporate and area levels;

III   development and application of:

- corporate bonus schemes,

- compensation practices for people on international and expatriate assignments.

IV   implementation of a consistent pension policy throughout the group and the provision of consulting advice.

4.   Management Communication

This function is concerned with:

I   communication of management policies and significant developments within the group;

II   provision of assistance or direction as required on special projects.

The principal medium of communication is the company magazine. Regular or special circulars, and the weekly newsletter are also used.

5. Integration and Surveillance

The department is also concerned with:

I developing, integrating and periodically assessing personnel programs to achieve corporate purpose, objectives, policies, and strategic shape;

II providing corporate management with an overview and periodic assessment of the key personnel functions throughout the group.

This is achieved by working together with area management on common problems, organizing such activities as area personnel officers meetings, etc.

Appendix P — Corporate Human Resource Function
— Description of Role
— Organization 4

This Appendix contains a description of the role of the corporate human resource function for Organization 4. The six areas are listed below.

1. The role is designed to forecast, conceptualize, plan for, and initiate programs on priority problems and emerging issues in the area of human resources by:

    - gathering information,

    - acquainting top management with needed changes and re-orientation,

    - developing relevant action programs in areas such as: legislation affecting the field, labour market characteristics, environmental trends, morale and attitudes, management continuity, optimal utilization of human resources, and conceptual and technical innovations in the field.

2. The role must ensure proper linkage of human resource planning with strategic planning. (The total business planning of the company needs to be connected to the human resource function to the same extent that it is linked to its financial and material resources.)

3. The role should conceptualize and enunciate the standards of performance for the human resource function, and be accountable for the professional quality of the function by:

    - developing overall human resource policies,

    - developing common procedures where necessary,

    - helping general managers use the human resource function,

    - acting within the framework of the job assignment process in hiring professional staff, and monitoring this development,

    - providing leadership to the professional staff,

    - monitoring and evaluating performance of the human resource function.

4. The role should build and maintain information systems based on relevant human resource issues.

5. The role must serve as company, business or professional representative in outside activities that are relevant to the field, and should be helpful in understanding and interpreting the environment of the company.

6. The role serves as adviser, counsellor to top management as needed, and assumes the distinctive responsibility of guiding senior management in human resource matters.

Appendix Q — Human Resource Planning Cycle — Organization 7

This Appendix describes the six stages of the human resource planning cycle for Organization 7.

Stage 1[1]

The vice presidents of both the corporate and the subsidiary's human resource groups develop appropriate overall concerns and goals for their organizational units. These are achieved by using their entity's strategic business objectives, as well as by employing information based on an analysis of internal and external environments.[2] The resulting concerns and associated strategic goals of each unit are given priority, based on near-term goals (12-18 months) and long-term goals (2-5 years).

Stage 2

The results of Stage 1 are used as the basis for an annual meeting of all the company's human resource professionals (the vice presidents and their staff) where total corporate human resource strategies (concerns, goals and priorities) are established. Such strategies are developed to show the overall human resource strategies that each subsidiary will use as a guide in the business planning process, along with the strategies unique to each subsidiary. Further, this planning session also considers near-term priorities and identifies potential areas for task- and work-sharing activities. Before priorities are established, each concern and goal is ranked in one of three categories:

- essential and cannot be deferred

- desirable and should be completed

- could be deferred

---

[1]   Reference to the various stages is to Exhibit 14 in Chapter VIII.

[2]   Examples of the results of this analysis are examined in Chapter IX.

Stage 3

The output of Stage 2 is used by the corporation and each subsidiary as a basis for developing business plans (5 years), stating specific objectives, actions, responsibilities, time frames, and effort. The output from Stage 3 is then used to present the human resource plan in each business plan, in accordance with corporate planning guidelines.

Stage 4

In this stage, the human resource business plans developed in Stage 3 are exchanged. The corporate human resource executive reviews and discusses with individual subsidiaries the adequacy of these plans and determines additional areas where synergy can be developed through better awareness of their respective activities.

Stage 5

Both the corporation and the subsidiaries formulate one-year human resource operating plans and allocate funds in accordance with corporate planning guidelines. Such plans become the basis for all related management for achievement action plans (the process whereby a manager and his subordinate: (a) clarify responsibilities, (b) establish short- and long-term objectives, and (c) evaluate current performance.

Stage 6

Implementation of the plans occurs following approval of the total operating plan and budget of the entities. The intercorporate personnel groups are responsible for a quarterly review of the progress of the entities and make adjustments to business and operating plans where circumstances have changed.

Integration with Overall Business Planning

Overall business planning is said to be integrated when the strategic objectives of each subsidiary correspond to the objectives of the head office. The subsidiary objectives and business plans developed in Stage 3 then become the basis for human resource inputs into the subsidiary's business planning process. The corporate human resource executive is then in a position to comment on the subsidiary's business plans relating to human resource content with a better knowledge of the subsidiary's human resource concerns and strategies.

Appendix R — Corporate Human Resources Strategic Issues and Goals — Organization 10

This Appendix presents three aspects of human resource planning in Organization 10. Part 1 contains the 1980 corporate human resource strategic issues; Part 2 contains examples of corporate human resource goals; Part 3 contains the 1981 corporate human resource strategic issues.

Part 1 — 1980 Corporate Human Resource Strategic Issues

1. Corporate Functional Capabilities

   - The function as a whole will be looked at from a quantitative and qualitative point of view to assess whether it is organized and staffed to manage the projected business growth objectives and environmental developments over the next five years.

2. Manpower

   - Projects will be undertaken to establish the company's long-term organizational and quantitative staffing needs to support its growth and profitability objectives.

   - Given the expected managerial environment in the '80s, the company's standards and measures of managerial performance will be continually assessed to ensure competent selection and performance.

3. Compensation and Benefits

   - Projects will be undertaken to reinforce individual performance by developing reward systems, which minimize tax impact and meet personal needs where possible.

   - Relocation policies will be improved to assist manpower planning and recruitment at site, regional, and international levels.

4. Employee Relations

   - The effectiveness of existing strategies, policies and programs for implementation of the company's management philosophy will be reviewed in the light of changing environmental and business factors.

Part 2 — Examples of Corporate Human Resource Goal Statements

Goal 1: Continue to improve the quality of senior manager/executive development and succession planning.

Goal 2: Determine future human resource requirements (5 to 10-year time frame) with particular emphasis on managerial and professional classifications, and prepare a plan for development, expansion, modification and development of the current pool of such employees to meet the corporate strategic and operational objectives.

Goal 3: Implement an improved performance appraisal rating system.

Goal 4: Develop recommendations on a total compensation policy for salaried employees in the United States and five European countries by July 1, 1980.

Goal 5: Revise or replace the company's Executive Incentive Program.

Part 3 — 1981 Corporate Human Resource Strategic Issues

In the plan period, people constitute a major concern. The concern is our ability to identify and develop enough qualified personnel to meet strategic growth plans on schedule.

We will need additional managers with business depth, but we will also need to develop more managers with broad skills to manage increasingly complex jobs with more interaction with the external environment. Criteria have been established for the "Manager of the '80s Project," and selection and training will be based on such criteria.

The human resource issues in this year's plan have been tested with a large cross section of XYZ managers using questionnaires, interviews and written responses. These managers have also participated in addressing the issues. The following summary is the direct result of their involvement.

Recruitment and Development

To meet growth needs and to overcome past conservative recruiting practices, future recruitment practices will recognize human resource needs in excess of short-term needs. Recruits will be younger, culturally diverse, and with a mix of disciplines geared for future needs. Emphasis will be placed on mobility and potential.

Useful entry positions will be established, and developmental, geographic and career moves will be executed earlier in employees' careers. Technical and other professional career ladders will be examined to provide paths for career specialists while those showing interest and ability as general managers will continue to be encouraged accordingly.

A more centrally directed approach will be needed to achieve an appropriate balance of skills to meet not only the needs of the individual departments but the future requirements of the company as well.

Rewards and Benefits

Reward and benefit programs will be adjusted to provide increased flexibility to meet individual needs of employees and their families. Specific attention will be given to providing rewards for risk-taking and innovation to reinforce the desire of the corporation to increase the level of innovation in all aspects of the company operation. Compensation systems will also be adjusted to reward short-term operating results as well as long-term strategic results.

Employee Mobility

Recruits, both in Canada and abroad, will be hired with an understanding that early mobility may be required, and development plans that include relocation will be established earlier in employees' careers. In support of relocation plans, expatriate compensation will be reviewed regularly to remain competitive.

Failure to achieve an increased level of mobility will necessitate a reconsideration of the company organizational structure, which is based on the assumption that key positions will be staffed from a total corporate pool.

Growth

The strategic growth plans are expected to stretch our management capabilities but it is felt that the strategic plans will be met with our complement of existing managers. Greater reliance will also have to be placed on younger managers, and the role of our experienced managers as mentors will be emphasized.

An aggressive recruitment plan will strengthen our inventory of future managers and accelerated development plans will equip existing managers for expected growth. It is also expected that managerial talent will be assimilated with the acquired companies, thus further diversifying XYZ's managerial expertise. The challenge will be to integrate and instruct such managers effectively. This process will be augmented with planned exchanges to key employees.

Non-managerial human resources will be acquired from an increasingly tight market. There will be an accelerated effort to recruit, augmented by plans to improve the efficiency of the current professional staff.

If all strategic growth options are exercised, it is estimated that by 1986 the current managerial/technical human resource population of 900 will grow by 50 per cent and the corporate staff group of 80 will grow by 35 per cent due to economies of scale.

Beyond the growth period, or in the absence of growth activity, a nominal increase of 2 per cent per year is planned in staff functions due to increasing demands from the external environment.

Future Organization Structure

A number of organizational design options have been developed to implement the succession plans for the senior executive. These options include regionalized and product-oriented structures and cover both executive and operating levels.

It is expected that recommendations will be made to the Management Committee in July 1981.

Appendix S — Corporate Personnel Strategy — Organization 2

This Appendix contains the corporate personnel strategy for Organization 2.[1]

1. **International Management Resources**

   Stemming from the strategic shape document for the corporation and the Management Committee's intention to give greater emphasis to corporate management of the personnel function, the following will be done:

   - specific identification of jobs and individuals, i.e.,

     (a) target positions to be staffed by international managers,

     (b) positions to be used to develop international managers,

     (c) individual candidates who have potential to develop "international management skills" or employees who already have acquired these skills,

   - development of related career progression programs,

   - development of special compensation policies, as required,

   - development of improved methods of re-entry.

2. **Overall Management Renewal**

   Changed requirements for management-level personnel in recent years have resulted in a reduced infusion of new blood into the organization. Using data from the succession planning exercise, the following will be reviewd:

   - whether such reduction has reached a point where it has become (or could become) a corporate issue;

   - and, if so, how far and how best can senior group management be involved in:

     (a) recruiting outside candidates

     (b) campus appearances

     (c) other

---

[1] This strategy document was presented to the Personnel Committee of the Board of Directors for information purposes.

3. **Innovation in "People Management"**

The company has lost momentum as an innovator in "people management." In order to regain our reputation as innovative, it is essential to have the active support of regional management for the Management Committee's desire to see innovation in "people management." Therefore, the following will be undertaken:

- periodic review at group management meetings (regional areas, etc.) of current innovations,

- promotion of exchange of information of these on-going innovations between operating locations during various inter-unit meetings,

- keeping abreast of new developments outside the company.

4. **Overall Group Personnel Management**

To assure implementation of the corporate Statement of Purpose, Objectives, Policies and Strategic Shape on personnel issues, the implementation of on-going reviews of personnel management approaches throughout the group will be undertaken. These reviews are intended to provide feedback to management.

5. **Health and Safety**

- *General*:

    With the objective of improving the corporation's overall performance, the following will be undertaken with assistance from managements of the various geographic areas.

    (a) to review the status of existing safety and occupational health programs in all company operating units,

    (b) to develop a schedule to establish programs where none exist,

    (c) to keep abreast of developments outside the company and the performance of similar companies or industries.

- *Safety*

    (a) fatalities: require immediate reporting by line management to executive vice president of the region; preparation of a basic accident report to the corporate safety committee,

(b) other accidents: require reviews twice a year by regional management on objectives and targets as well as actual performance.

- *Health*

    To promote better standards, an exchange of information on current health standards throughout the group will be undertaken.

Appendix T — Human Resource Function — Division of Authority — Organization 8

This Appendix presents an analysis of the division of authority between the corporate and divisional human resource functions for Organization 8.

Corporate Human Resources

- Development of policies and programs in response to identified issues and trends necessary for corporate integrity

- Operating corporate programs where it is not efficient to delegate to the next level

- Consultation and staff services for corporate management and divisional human resource departments

- Monitoring/auditing divisional human resource performance as a diagnostic feed-back loop

Divisional Human Resources

- Administration and control of corporate policies and programs within the division

- Development and implementation of policies and programs to meet localized and/or divisional needs, which do not jeopardize corporate integrity

- Consultation and staff services for divisional management

- Identification of issues and trends through diagnosis of particular geographic or divisional environments

Appendix U — Employee Relations Function — Division of Authority — Organization 3

Part 1 — Corporate Employee Relations Function

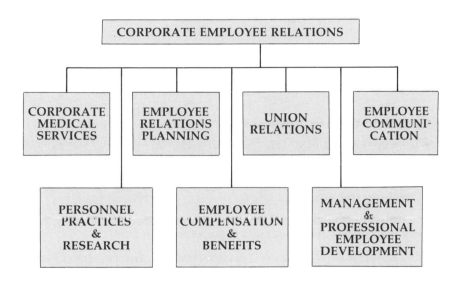

| CORPORATE EMPLOYEE RELATIONS |
| CORPORATE MEDICAL SERVICES | EMPLOYEE RELATIONS PLANNING | UNION RELATIONS | EMPLOYEE COMMUNICATION |
| PERSONNEL PRACTICES & RESEARCH | EMPLOYEE COMPENSATION & BENEFITS | MANAGEMENT & PROFESSIONAL EMPLOYEE DEVELOPMENT |

Operating Work	Staff Work
• Union Relations Master Agreement Negotiations — Negotiation Administration — 3rd Stage Grievance Hearing — Arbitration • Organization and Executive Manpower • Administration of Corporate Staff Compensation	• Policy Development • Practices and Instructions • Research • Counsel to Operating Management • Development of Company-Wide Employee Relations Programs, e.g. — Employee Communication — Employee Communication — Toxic Materials Management — Environmental Protection — Salary Planning Systems — Human Resources Information Systems

Source: Organization 3; The Conference Board of Canada.

Part 2 — Plant Level Employee Relations Function

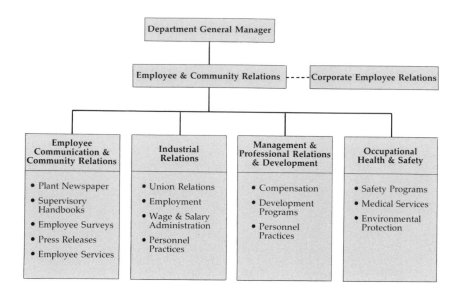

Department General Manager

Employee & Community Relations ----- Corporate Employee Relations

Employee Communication & Community Relations
- Plant Newspaper
- Supervisory Handbooks
- Employee Surveys
- Press Releases
- Employee Services

Industrial Relations
- Union Relations
- Employment
- Wage & Salary Administration
- Personnel Practices

Management & Professional Relations & Development
- Compensation
- Development Programs
- Personnel Practices

Occupational Health & Safety
- Safety Programs
- Medical Services
- Environmental Protection

Appendix V —External Environmental Analysis, 1979-83 — Organization 7

This appendix contains sample forms for an external environmental analysis exercise from one of the participating organizations. Examples of environmental issues have been taken from the four domains of environmental analysis: economic/monetary, technological, political, and social/cultural.

Domain: Economic/Monetary

1. TRENDS: _North American rates of inflation will be at 8-10 per cent per yr. Fuel and other essential imports will continue to put heavy pressure on dollar exchange rates relative to other major currencies._

    PROBABLE IMPACT ON COMPANY: _Domestic markets will be sluggish, resulting in increased competition. Offshore markets could benefit from lower dollar exchange rates, but competition from Germany and Japan will be tougher — including their attempts to penetrate our domestic markets._

    PROBABLE IMPACT ON HUMAN RESOURCE POLICY AND PROCEDURES/ACTIONS:
    — Shift to more entrepreneurial style
    — Involvement in new acquisition evaluation/orientation
    — Less uniformity-increased information needs

2. TRENDS: _government cost and intervention_

    PROBABLE IMPACT ON COMPANY: _Increased costs — compliance measurements/control/reporting_
    — loss of management flexibility

    PROBABLE IMPACT ON HUMAN RESOURCE POLICY AND PROCEDURES/ACTIONS:
    — decentralize procedures/practices
    — greater involvement in proposed legislation review/appeal
    — increased involvement in business planning

Domain: Technological

1. TRENDS: *Market competition creating demand for both improved product performance and total cost, which in turn creates demand for increased rate of technological change with resulting increase in R & D expense.*

    PROBABLE IMPACT ON COMPANY: *Decreased ability to respond due to:*
    — *potential increase in ratio of failure to success*
    — *availability of adequate funding*
    — *availability of skilled human resources*

    PROBABLE IMPACT ON HUMAN RESOURCE POLICY AND PROCEDURES/ACTIONS:
    — *improved manpower planning and development*
    — *increased involvement in productivity/motivation improvement*
    — *increased involvement in employee/labour relations and problems in displacement of jobs — compensation inflation*

Domain: Political

1. TRENDS: *Increased social legislation by federal and provincial/state legislatures; increasing employee expectations in involvement in manpower process.*

    PROBABLE IMPACT ON COMPANY: *Decreasing flexibility and control of business due to:*
    — *policies being externally driven*
    — *increased unionization*
    — *threat of management unionization*

    PROBABLE IMPACT ON HUMAN RESOURCE POLICY AND PROCEDURES/ACTIONS:
    — *improve management and employee relations*
    — *develop strategies to optimize current strengths*

2. TRENDS: *Resistance to multinationals' penetration of domestic markets by local politicians/businessmen.*

    PROBABLE IMPACT ON COMPANY: *Increased need for licensing and joint ventures to enter offshore markets.*

    PROBABLE IMPACT ON HUMAN RESOURCE POLICY AND PROCEDURES/ACTIONS:
    — *Potential labour relations problems*
    — *Demand for improved management development programs in technology/joint venture management*

Domain: Social/Cultural

1. TRENDS: *Increasing demands by consumer groups/taxpayers to restrict growth and control costs of goods and services, through regulatory hearings, etc.*

   PROBABLE IMPACT ON COMPANY: *Slower growth/replacement budgets of organizations serviced resulting in lower earnings and cutbacks in R & D.*

   PROBABLE IMPACT ON HUMAN RESOURCE POLICY AND PROCEDURES/ACTIONS:
   — *Improved compensation planning/administration control*
   — *Increased productivity*
   — *Innovative collective labour agreement negotiations*

2. TRENDS: *Continuing trend for disenchantment of academics/students with business and low enrolments in science/engineering programs.*

   PROBABLE IMPACT ON COMPANY: *Shortage of competent/current knowledge workers.*

   PROBABLE IMPACT ON HUMAN RESOURCE POLICY AND PROCEDURES/ACTIONS:
   — *Increased liaison with colleges/students*
   — *Adoption of more effective intern programs*
   — *Restructuring of jobs to provide challenge/responsibility*
   — *Promotion of corporate social awareness*

Appendix W — Monitoring the Internal Environment — An Example

This appendix is from an organization that employs a variety of approaches for monitoring the internal environment. The description below is a summarized version of material provided to all employees.

1. The Role of Communication

One of the reasons for our success over the years is our willingness and ability to communicate with our employees. Through communication, we are able to understand and address the job related concerns and problems of our employees. It enables managers and employees to set priorities in accomplishing their tasks and work towards mutually satisfactory goals. Continued success of the organization will depend on good communication and good employee relations.

What constitutes good communication? First and foremost, there must be a two-way flow of information and opinion. It must give both the employee and the manager a chance to talk *and* listen. In our organization, the entire employee/manager relationship is based on two-way communication with built-in channels of appeal.

2. Important Employee Relations Fundamentals

Two important fundamentals are embodied in our employee relations practice:

(a) Basic beliefs of the organization:

> We have three basic beliefs: (1) respect for the individual, (2) best possible customer service, and (3) every task performed in a superior way. These beliefs are long standing and affect every management decision. These beliefs are an essential part of our personnel policies and practices.

(b) Managing Human Resources:

> Our personnel philosophy is founded on the premise that line management is responsible for implementing and operating personnel programs and policies. Every manager is a personnel manager. They recruit, train, evaluate performance, recommend pay increases, and develop employees in their jobs. The company stresses the employee/manager rela-

tionship above all else. The role of the personnel department is to identify needs, develop programs, and train managers in implementing personnel programs and monitoring these services.

3. Overall Management Communication System

The overall management communication system in the organization is shown in the accompanying diagram. The system starts with senior management who are responsible for pursuing the company's fundamental philosophy (upper left box).

The communication of personnel policies and practices that flow from this philosophy is the responsibility of line management. The development of programs to do this is the responsibility of the personnel department.

Management Communication System

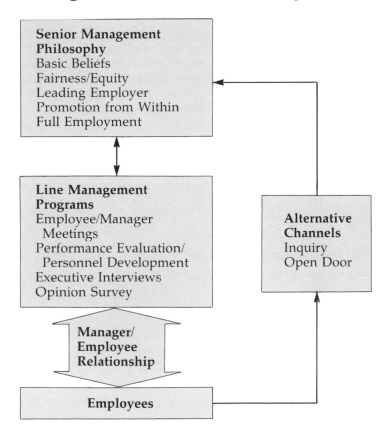

There are a number of such programs. They are all designed to reinforce the employee/manager relationship. Sound employee relations is the goal of the communication system. Some of the programs accomplish this on an individual basis. Examples are:

- Performance evaluation and personal development

- Executive interviews — This program provides every employee with an opportunity to meet with his manager's manager to discuss any aspect of his job.

Other programs require a manager to meet with all the employees in a department at one time. Examples are:

- Employee/manager meetings — These are quarterly meetings designed to provide an opportunity for employees to engage in a dialogue on items of specific interest to them. In addition, the manager is expected to communicate information regarding the company.

- Employee opinion surveys. — The objective of the survey, which is conducted company-wide every 18 months, is to foster improvements in the company as a place to work and in the operation of the business, by measuring employee satisfaction and assessing employee attitudes.

The successful use of these programs depends on thorough management training. We have a wide variety of training programs for both new and existing managers, which are designed to enable them to discuss their issues and concerns.

The communication system also has checks or alternative channels built in to ensure communication is working. There are two such channels:

- A program exists that provides a vehicle for an employee to question, challenge, or comment on any company, job or personnel-related subject. Employees who use this program know their anonymity is guaranteed, and that a written reply will be received. This program, called "Inquiry," was started 15 years ago and is actively used.

- An open door policy is in place to provide an employee with an opportunity to see his or her senior manager or any other executive to register a job-related concern.

These two programs allow employees to express concerns openly or anonymously about any aspect of their work situation. This employee right is carefully protected by senior management who pay special attention to these two feed-back programs.

Summary

Our monitoring and communication system has been in place for many years and new programs have been added as the environment has changed. The system has proven that it is capable of responding to changes. Given its fundamental approach it should continue to respond to the needs of our employees and our business.